THE
NARON

NARON FAMILY IN HUT

NARON HUTS

The woman in the centre is the daughter of a Nama chief and a Naron woman.

From photographs taken at Sandfontein by J. Drury *of the S.A. Museum.*

THE
NARON

A BUSHMAN TRIBE OF THE
CENTRAL KALAHARI

by

D. F. BLEEK

HON. LECTURER ON BUSHMAN LANGUAGE
TO THE UNIVERSITY OF
CAPE TOWN

CAMBRIDGE
AT THE UNIVERSITY PRESS
1928

CAMBRIDGE UNIVERSITY PRESS
Cambridge, New York, Melbourne, Madrid, Cape Town,
Singapore, São Paulo, Delhi, Tokyo, Mexico City

Cambridge University Press
The Edinburgh Building, Cambridge CB2 8RU, UK

Published in the United States of America by Cambridge University Press, New York

www.cambridge.org
Information on this title: www.cambridge.org/9781107647015

First published 1928
Re-issued 2011

A catalogue record for this publication is available from the British Library

ISBN 978-1-107-64701-5 Paperback

PREFACE

THIS is the first of a series of short studies on South African tribes, which the School of African Life and Languages will publish from time to time as material and funds permit. The series will comprise the result of original research in the organisation, language or special cultural feature of the native races of South Africa.

It is a source of great satisfaction to the Publication Committee that they are able to commence the series with so valuable an account of a Bushman tribe and under the honoured name of Bleek.

Miss Bleek will also be responsible for the second number to be published shortly, *A Comparative Vocabulary of Bushman Languages*. A third number on the Nama Hottentots by Mrs A. W. Hoernle, now lecturer in Social Anthropology at the University of the Witwatersrand, is in course of preparation. These will be followed by studies of different Bantu tribes, the result of intensive research by students and independent workers, such as is being conducted under the general supervision of the School. The funds available from the University will not permit of the publication of larger monographs in this series. But it is hoped that these small volumes will to some extent make good the still serious deficit in our knowledge of the native races of South Africa.

T. T. BARNARD

UNIVERSITY OF CAPE TOWN
August 1927

CONTENTS

INTRODUCTION.

In the latter half of 1920 the Government of the South-West Protectorate asked the South African Museum at Cape Town to organize an expedition to do anthropological research work among the Bushmen of the Protectorate. Two gentlemen from the Museum went up to do the physical research work, such as taking casts, measurements, etc., and I, though unconnected with the Museum, was asked to undertake the philological research.

On the advice of Dr Fourie, Medical Officer of Health of the Protectorate, the Government placed the empty police station of Sandfontein on the border of the Bechuanaland Protectorate at our disposal. It is in the Bushman country, on the boundary between the territory of two tribes, the Naron and the ||k'au ||en, or Auen, as they are generally called by Europeans who cannot pronounce the clicks.

After a month's work at Windhoek among the Bushmen prisoners in the jail, we started for Sandfontein, which we reached in the first days of January 1921. A number of families of both tribes were in residence near the police station. Our nearest European neighbours were fifteen miles distant. A Klip Kaffir constable, Saul, was detailed as guide and interpreter, as he had grown up near Sandfontein, spoke the Naron language well, and could understand the ||k'au ||en tongue fairly.

I stayed at Sandfontein till March, the last six weeks alone with the Bushmen and my interpreter. During that time the Bushmen became more confidential, and as I began to understand and speak their languages, I obtained a good deal of information. Still, I regretted leaving just as I was getting into the swing of my work, and was very glad when the Government asked me to return next summer. I reached Sandfontein at the beginning of November 1921, this time without an interpreter, and stayed there till the middle of March 1922. The report I sent in to the Government of the Protectorate in September 1922 forms the basis of this study, which is now being published with their leave by the University of Cape Town.

DISTRIBUTION.

1. Naron is the name by which one tribe of Bushmen at Sand-fontein call themselves. They also know the name of ||aikwe, which, however, seems to be used by those of their tribe who live farther to the east. Beyond them again to the east or north-east live the Tsaukwe, Tsɔrokwe and !giŋkwe, all friendly tribes whose language the Naron understand, to whom they give the collective name of k″am-ka-kwe, mouth's people.

Passarge calls the group Aikwe, from ||aikwe, also Kalahari Bushmen; I call them the Central Group of Bushmen. The territory of the group is roughly wedge shaped, the apex of the wedge being at Oas. The north-east boundary is formed by the Oas-Ngami road, the southern boundary a line from Oas to Palapye on the Rhodesian Railway, the base seems indeterminate. The Naron speak a language closely related to Nama; it has four clicks, has the grammatical formation of the Hottentot tongues, with similar endings for gender and number, and the same topsy turvy structure of the sentence. The vocabulary has many roots in common with Nama, yet there are sufficient differences between the two to call them two languages of one group, rather than two dialects of one language. Judging from lists of words published by Passarge, Seiner and Norton, the other members of this group all speak dialects closely related to Naron. Tati in Southern Rhodesia has a Bushman tribe, whose language is a link between this group and the following.

2. The Northern Group of Bushmen comprise the ||k′au ||en or ǂau ||en, residing north of Oas and west of the Oas-Ngami road, and the !kuŋ or !kũ, generally called Kung, occupying the territory between the ||k′au ||en country and the Okavango River. Passarge calls these tribes Ngami Bushmen, also Aukwe.

The linguistic difference between this group and the Central Group is distinct.

The tribes of the Northern Group speak dialects of one language which is distantly related to the following, the Southern Group. It has the same sequence of words as the latter, and similar pronouns, but has some distinct variations in grammar, and a different vocabulary. It has also only four clicks, like Nama.

3. The Southern Group is represented in the South-West Protectorate by the |nu ||en, called by white men the Nusan. This tribe lives between the Black Nossop and the eastern border of the Protectorate, south of Oas. The best-known representatives of this group are the |xam-ka !ke or Bushmen of the Cape Colony, but other branches are found in Griqualand West and Gordonia, in the southern part of Bechuanaland, and the lower Nossop, and at Lake Chrissie in the Eastern Transvaal.

One distinguishing feature of the languages spoken by these tribes is the use of the fifth or labial click. They have a strong resemblance in grammar, and the vocabularies show many common roots.

4. West of the Black Nossop and the border of the Auen and Kung territory, which is approximately on the 19th degree of longitude, scattered about among other natives and white settlers are the Hei ||kum or Nama-Bushmen, so called because they have lost their original tongue and only speak Nama, much as the Klip Kaffirs do, with whom they often mix. From all I hear the Bushmen of the sea coast have likewise lost their native speech and only know Nama. Hei ||kum means "Bush sleepers."

During my stay at Sandfontein on the eastern border of the Protectorate, I was daily in close touch with Auen and Naron, that is with the members of the Northern and Central Groups. On my way back, a deviation to the south brought me into contact with a number of Nusan, and at Windhoek jail I had the opportunity of interrogating various Kung and Hei ||kum Bushmen. The Naron were in the majority at Sandfontein, and I thought it best to devote most time to them, because a fair amount of literature has already been published about the Kung and the Auen, namely:

"Translation of !kuŋ Texts," by Miss Lloyd in *Specimens of Bushmen Folklore*, by Bleek and Lloyd, 1911.

"Grundriss einer Grammatik der Buschmannsprache vom Stamm der !kũ Buschmänner," von H. Vedder, Missioner, published in the *Zeitschrift für Kolonial Sprachen*, Band I, Heft 1, 1910–11.

"Die Auén; Ein Beitrag zur Buschmannforschung," von Hans Kaufmann, in *Mitteilungen aus den Deutschen Schutzgebieten*, Band 23, Heft 3, 1910.

"Die Bastard Buschleute der Nord-Kalahari," von Franz Seiner, in *Mitteilungen aus den Deutschen Schutzgebieten*, Band 26, Heft 3, 1913.

I will therefore begin with a review of Naron habits, customs, and beliefs, then state shortly in what points I have found the other tribes to differ from them, and conclude with a grammatical sketch of the languages.

MODE OF LIFE.

The Naron live in small divisions or hordes. Each horde has its own territory, a very large piece of country with more than one water-hole. Its borders are invisible to the white man's eye, but well known to the people themselves, who shift about in gypsy fashion all over their own land, without trespassing on their neighbours' territory, though single persons occasionally pay a short visit across the border, mostly for trading purposes.

Their movements are regulated by the supplies of food and water. When they have eaten up all the fruit and roots in one place, they go to another; they have different summer and winter quarters. They are nomads—yet cling to the soil. The people at Sandfontein begged me to stay, so that they might go on earning tobacco and clothes; but it was in vain to tell them of places near Gobabis where they could earn all they wanted. They would not budge from their country. Only to follow a well-known and trusted master will they move far outside their border and then not for long.

Their little clusters of huts are generally found near a water-hole, that is within walking distance of it, not more than an hour or two's march distant. They do not live at the water itself for fear of frightening away the game, which is most easily shot or trapped as it comes to drink.

All the families drinking at one water may live in one group, or there may be several lots of huts in different directions. Sometimes I have seen three or four huts together, sometimes twenty, with about sixty to eighty inhabitants. Every few weeks a new hut appears, or a vacant space shows where one has gone.

As the village is such a fluctuating quantity, it is difficult to estimate the numbers of a horde or tribe. Each hut has from two to five inmates: man, wife and from one to three children are found in many, or an old couple alone, or girls who are too old to share with their parents. An old widower may live alone or with a boy; a widow and her little ones are generally quartered with the girls. If no older woman is with them, the girls' hut stands near that of their parents, to whom they creep back if there is a bad thunder-storm, I am told. The bigger boys and young bachelors sleep under a tree. In very wet weather their mothers build them a hut.

The women do all the building here. The men may cut a few branches, but their wives plant them in the ground in a semi-circle, tie the tops together with a thong or bark fibre, put smaller sticks in between them, and thatch the whole with grass, making a cosy little wind screen. In bad weather chunks of wood are often laid on top to keep the grass in place. The size, and the care with which a hut is built, vary with the season: in dry weather a very slight shelter suffices, just a little sloping screen, perhaps made by sticking grass in the branches of a bush. As the rainy season ap-proaches a proper semicircular hut is made, from four to five feet high, the opening to leeward of course, and when the rain really comes, the half circle is increased to about a three-quarter circle, often thereby changing the direction of the opening in accordance with the different wind. There is no door; the opening is about four feet high. The floor is partly covered with grass, which is often changed. Some families have a spare skin to lay on top of the grass. Ostrich eggshells, a wooden mortar and perhaps an empty paint tin form the furniture. Sometimes a reed mat, used for sifting ants, is found rolled up and stuck into the roof. No family owns more than its members can carry.

The neighbourhood of the huts is kept fairly clean. Gnawed bones are thrown on a pile, then carried out to the bushes by the women, who also sweep their huts out with a branch, and clear up any mess made by the little children. No dirt is allowed any-where near the village. In front of each hut is the fireplace, a heap of ashes, from the height of which one can estimate the length of residence in that spot. At night a second little fire is made just inside the door opening, and the inmates sleep round it, nearly in it, in cold weather. These ashes are swept up every morning and added to the heap outside.

FIRES AND FOOD.

To save the trouble of lighting a fresh fire at night, glowing embers are covered over before the Bushmen leave the camp. If one family's fire goes out, they fetch a stick from the neighbours. When no fire is obtainable, they lay a piece of soft wood on the ground, make a pointed hole in it, sharpen the end of a hard stick, insert it into the hole and twirl it rapidly, holding the lower stick with a foot or knee. They put some fine dry grass close to the point of contact to catch the spark, and have more grass and twigs handy to carry on the fire. Both sticks must be very dry. Bushmen going on long journeys carry a couple with them, also dry grass or a bit of soft bird's nest to take its place.

Their methods of cooking vary. Wild cucumbers, nuts, bulbs, and many bits of meat are baked in the ashes. A bright fire is made and allowed to die down, a hole is scraped in the ashes, the food put in and covered over.

Some specially dainty kinds of meat are roasted on the end of a pointed stick which leans over the fire. Other bits of meat, stamped locusts or tsama seeds and foods obtained from white men, such as mealie meal, are cooked with water in a tin. Formerly they bought earthen pots from the Auen or Bechuana, but to-day old paint tins or jam tins have replaced them. Both men and women cook, but more often the latter, who also stamp many kinds of seeds, berries and leaves in the wooden mortars with stone bottoms made by the Auen. Wooden spoons and plates are sometimes to be seen, also purchased outside the tribe, and half tortoise-shells too are used. The ostrich breast bone, though well known to the older men as a dish, is rarely seen now. But for carrying water the ostrich eggshell still holds its own. Gemsbok stomachs or the skin of the spring hare used to be in vogue as water bags, but are seldom to be seen nowadays. The lower opening of the stomach is tied tightly with sinew, the upper used as a spout and fastened in between whiles. To make a water bag of a spring hare skin, they cut off the head, slit along each leg and pull the skin off whole; then tie the hind legs together, cut off the fore legs, tie the neck opening so as to make it smaller and blow the whole up.

They eat three times a day both meat and other food, when obtainable, but very often now there is no meat, as the game laws get stricter every year. The people are gradually being forced into a vegetarian diet, against their will.

Anteaters, ant bears, tortoises, porcupines, bull frogs and locusts are welcome additions to their menu, and the wilder Bushmen are said to eat snakes, especially the larger kinds. They cut off the head and roast the bodies. Leopard and lynx are eaten on the rare occasions when they are caught, but not the hyena, nor the baboon, the latter on account of its being so like a man. Anthropophagy is unknown even in cases of great hunger.

They are very fond of honey and young bees, also of the male ants, when these fly out after rain. Of course game is their favourite food, when they get a chance at it—and hare, spring hare, guinea fowl, knorhaan, paauw and ostrich are a great delight. The eggs of these birds and a number of small birds are eaten too.

Still all these are not easily obtained. They depend for their existence on the wild vegetable food, which varies with the season. In October or November with the first rains numbers of bulbs come up, wild onions of all sorts and the roots of an orchid. The little green cucumber is also found, which is a standing dish right through till winter. In December and January the *Grewia* berries ripen and become the staple food of the community. Some are eaten as picked, stone and all, others stamped in the mortar and swallowed uncooked. A kind of sorrel leaf is treated in the same way. It is said to be good for the digestion. As these go over, the "saut bessies" (*Grewia* sp.), cucumbers, tubers come in, besides which other roots are still eaten. Then the ground nuts come in and more wild bulbs, which seem to flourish through the winter.

But as the sun turns back and spring comes, food becomes very scarce; people must walk far to get a meal and grow lean, till the first rain falls and there is plenty again. If that rain does not come, then the scarcity is great, and they often have to go away to distant parts of their land and the weaklings, old and young, perish.

At the end of the report I append a list of the botanical names of plants used for food, etc., the flowers and fruit of which were obtainable at Sandfontein in summer. Most of them were collected by Miss Wilman, Curator of the McGregor Museum, Kimberley, who had them all classified and supplied me with the proper designations. I obtained the Bushman names and uses. Other food plants could not be identified as they were not in flower.

It does not seem as if many taboos in the food line still existed. Paauw meat and ostrich eggs are chiefly given to old men as the greatest delicacies. Some say young children, or girls till they have had their first baby, are not to eat steenbok, lest they remain small, but others tell me that all meat is eaten by everyone. Honey touched by a baboon must not be eaten, else you will die.

DRESS.

All the Naron and Auen I have seen wear clothes, but I have been told by three different Europeans that they have come upon Bushmen in the wilder parts of both Auen and Naron districts either without any clothes or with only a kaross, no apron. This is confirmed by several old men at Sandfontein as being practised far away to the north and east by quite wild clans not living near permanent water.

The men's clothing consists of a three-cornered skin apron, two ends of which are tied round the waist, while the third is drawn between the legs and tied behind, and a skin cloak or kaross, generally made of a single duiker skin. A few have a larger kaross made from the skin of a young gemsbok or harte-beest cow. When travelling or seeking food, a round leather bag is slung on over the right shoulder, hanging on the left hip, and a long bag, made of a single steenbok skin, is hung over the left shoulder to carry their weapons in. Occasionally men have a net of sinew slung from both shoulders in which to carry a large load. They make these nets themselves, rolling the sinew on the thigh, and then knotting it. When unused, the net rolls into a small compass and goes easily into the long bag. A few men sport leather sandals and a skin cap. For running down game a small half sandal with downward curving point is used.

The round bag is also worn by women. Both sexes carry in it, or attached to the kaross, a tiny leather tobacco pouch, now often replaced by a trade tobacco bag.

The women wear a hanging apron in front, which may be either a semicircular piece of leather, or a number of bead or leather tassels attached to a belt. The girls more often wear the latter, the married women the former, but there is no hard and fast rule. Young girls have only a small kaross, like those of the men. Matrons also wear a larger skin apron behind, sometimes hanging from the shoulders, more often tied round the waist, almost meeting over or under the apron in front, and a large kaross made with several leather strings by which they tie the top over the right and under the left shoulder, and the middle round the waist, forming a convenient fold under the left arm. In this they carry ostrich eggshells filled with water, roots and fruit, grass or firewood, and the baby on top. It is wonderful what a load they can bear.

Men make the clothes. First they tan the skins, i.e. scrape them, rub them, fold and dance on them, leave them in the sand for hours, and rub in a mixture of fat and red clay. Then they sew them with sinew, using metal borers to prick the holes through which the sinew is threaded. A young man on marrying must present his wife with a full-sized woman's kaross, for which purpose he must obtain six steenbok skins, or a whole gemsbok or hartebeest skin, generally that of a cow. Such a kaross will last for several years, but must be occasionally replaced, and the petticoat, apron and round bag are also in demand. Here again the game laws[1] press very hard on those clans who do not live near farms and have no opportunity of getting clothes by their labour.

Save for a trifling ornament babies go naked till about ten or twelve months old; then the boys are given a tiny belt with a semicircular flap of leather in front, the girls an apron of tassels. Their mother's kaross continues to be their sole protection from the cold till they are weaned, when about three or four years old. The little girls then receive a tiny kaross hanging from the shoulders. Judging from appearances I should say that a piece of a grown-up's worn-out garment is used. The boys now wear an apron like those of the men, but no cloak of any sort till they are in their teens and are taken out to learn hunting. At night they crouch close to the fire or snuggle up to their elders.

ORNAMENTS.

All women and children and the younger men wear ornaments. Ostrich eggshell beads of various sizes are the oldest Bushman ornament. They are made by the women. With a stone the eggshell is broken into small pieces. These are pierced with an iron awl bought from Europeans or Ovambos, and then threaded on to a strip of sinew. The chain thus made is laid on the thigh or kaross, and the rough edges are chipped off with a horn. Then the women twist soft fibre from under the bark of some trees between the beads, making the chain very taut, and afterwards grind down the edges with a grooved stone.

These beads are used as single chains or worked into more complicated ornaments. Bands of them are worn on the hair, sometimes encircling the whole head, more often tied to the hair on either side, while a long narrow strip of beads may hang down

[1] Under the present Government of the South-West Protectorate no game may be shot without a licence, costing £1 for each season.

the forehead or on to the neck behind. Necklaces and bracelets of beads are to be seen, and very long chains of larger beads are fastened three or four times round the waist.

Women's and girls' aprons are sometimes trimmed with beads. In fact women wear as many as they can possibly obtain. Young men never have so many, but do not disdain them. I have often seen a youth with a nice coronet of beads.

Trade beads are not unknown and are often mixed with the others in making ornaments. I have seen girls with two chains of small glass beads tied to the hair, falling at either side of the face. They also wear various spicy roots suspended from the neck, partly as a charm, partly to nibble from.

Young men burn fancy patterns into the pipe sticks they wear suspended round the neck. The older men scorn ornaments but often have a plain pipe stick or a knife slung on a leather thong round the neck and have plain leather bands below the knee and round the arm above the biceps. The latter are worn by women and young people in addition to their other gear. Cowries are prized as ornaments, but are rare.

All possessions are worn daily, not kept for special occasions. Women prize them highly, and as they grow old hand them down to their daughters. Eggshell beads are not buried with a woman; her people keep them.

Paint and Tattoo.

The Naron adorn themselves with black and red paint. The black is charcoal, the red is clay brought from afar; both are mixed with fat. The mixture is rubbed on with a finger chiefly over the eyes, on the cheekbone and round the mouth. Young women and girls get themselves up thus for a dance and occasionally the young men paint too. Girls going to be married or desirous of being married smear red paint round the eyes.

Both sexes are tattooed by making slight incisions about an inch long into the skin and rubbing ash black into the wounds. Women are tattooed for ornament only on the face, thighs and buttocks. An old woman is the operator; she cuts them at any convenient time during their childhood or girlhood and receives a present for doing so. Both thighs are never cut on one occasion.

Very frequently one sees women with a black stripe tattooed down the centre of the forehead, one or two horizontal ones at the corners of the eyes, and a whole forest of slanting cuts on the buttocks and outside of the thighs. I asked an old woman why they had themselves tattooed. "That the men may see us pretty," was her reply.

Men have three kinds of cuts. First the vertical one, two or three between the eyebrows given to big boys at their initiation ceremony. These are about half an inch long. Powdered acid roots are rubbed into the wound to keep it from closing as it heals, but no colouring matter is applied. All Kung, Auen or Naron men and big lads that I have seen have these cuts. They are said to be given to make the lads see well, i.e. give them good luck in shooting, but are evidently a tribal mark connected with their religion. The Southern Bushmen do not have them.

These cuts are often half covered by a real tattoo mark—a dark stripe down the middle of the forehead similar to those worn by women. Many men have it, also horizontal tattoo marks at the corners of the eyes. These, I believe, are for purposes of ornament, though it is difficult in their language to distinguish between "seeing well" and "looking nice." Medicine men make these cuts, which are optional, in return for a present.

Thirdly, one finds on any part of a man's body, especially on the arms and chest, less *voyant* tattoo marks, or cuts; in the older ones the colour has often faded. Old men tattoo a successful hunter in return for an offering of game in order to give him good luck in finding the next buck. These cuts are optional. I have seen a noted hunter, an old man, who had only three; but as a rule the seniors manage to instil such a fear of a run of ill luck into the younger men that there is rarely a buck shot of which they do not get the titbits. Besides these the biceps muscle of the foreleg is given, a tiny bit of which is burnt to ashes and rubbed into the cut.

These tattoo marks are not so dark as those on the face made by medicine men, probably for ornament. The Auen have all the tattoo marks mentioned above. The Nusan make a few tattoo marks for ornament only, generally at the corners of the eyes, women also on the legs. This is not done by medicine men.

A few men and women pierce the ears with a metal needle, and wear ear-rings purchased from the Bechuana.

As far as I can ascertain, no other operations are performed on either men or women. Circumcision is unknown, and the women deny that any operation is performed on the girls, though I have heard of such with another tribe.

Rubbing the face and body with fat and powdering with buchu is done by old and young. It is their method of washing. I have seen a woman pick up some tiny nutty berries, crack the shell, crush the kernels in her palm, spit on them and rub face and neck with the greasy mess. She certainly looked the better for it. Many women carry small tortoise-shells filled with powdered buchu, with a bit of soft bird's nest, or else of jackal's skin stuck in the top as a puff, and powder their face and body.

There are half a dozen aromatic herbs at Sandfontein all called by the Hottentot name for "buchu." Some are given in the Appendix.

Real washing with water is only done by those Bushmen who have been much with Europeans. In spite of this, a Bushman rarely smells unpleasant, unless he wears European clothing.

His own leather dress or undress is not odoriferous. Unwashed linen and woollen is of course soon unpleasant, but even then the Bushman has not the rank smell so easily given out by the black races, though most of them far surpass him in personal cleanliness.

Hair and Beard.

The Narons' hair varies. Some have proper "peppercorns" like Colonial Bushmen, others a woollier crop. Some women un-curl the little clusters of hair and roll them out with fat, so that they hang down a couple of inches, making a fringe round the head. Otherwise the hair is not dressed at all, but occasionally the whole or part of the head is shaved to get rid of the lice. Old women generally act as barbers. I have seen one good dame trimming a youth's hair round neck and forehead. She sat on the ground with his head in her lap, and shaved him with a scrap of tin about an inch long, which she stropped on her hard old hand. Needless to say no soap and water were used.

All the babies I have seen had a thick crop of hair even when only a week old, but I am told that bald babies are not infrequent. The little one's hair has a tendency to grow far down on the fore-head and into the neck. To prevent this, mothers smear a band of red clay and fat round the edge of the hair.

Men do not grow beards much before forty, and then have only a very small fringe on lip and chin, about a quarter of an inch long. About seventy, a slight iron grey shading is visible; real white heads are rare, as indeed really old Naron are rare. The women seem to die off at about fifty to sixty, the men wear better. I estimate that a number of those I saw were from sixty to seventy-five, but only one octogenarian. I am not judging by appearances, but by relative ages and other data.

I know that a general impression exists that Bushmen live to a great age, but in my experience this is mostly based on mistakes. Some middle-aged farmer states: "This man must be at least a hundred, he was quite old when I was a boy." Probably the Bushman was then thirty-five to forty and much wrinkled, and is now seventy or eighty. Almost every Bushman here and elsewhere presented to me as being exceptionally old proved on investigation to be twenty to thirty years younger than supposed. The women in particular look eighty when from the age of their children one can tell they are not above fifty-five to sixty.

WEAPONS.

The Narons' chief weapon is the bow and arrow. Bows are about a yard to a yard and a half long, are made of the wood of the *Grewia* and strung with sinew or home-made string. Sinew bows are counted the better ones. The ends of the wood are tightly bound round with sinew bands to prevent them splitting. Into the band on the upper end a small leather catch is tied, which prevents the bow-string from slipping when hitched over it. Sometimes a band of sinew is wound round the middle of the bow.

Arrows are of two kinds, the older tipped with bone, the more modern with iron. The shafts are reeds which only grow in certain places, as at Rietfontein. The shaft is one and a half to two feet long, bound at the end with flat grass. The bone arrow-head, six to ten inches long and a quarter inch in diameter, is split off the foreleg of an ostrich or kudu, heated, then pared down at one end to a sharp point, at the other it is rounded off. Both ends can fit into the reed. For safety in carrying, the poisoned sharp point is turned in; for shooting, the arrow-head is reversed, the blunt end turned in.

The iron-headed arrow is not reversible. It is called the "male" arrow, though the bone arrow is not called the female. The metal for these heads is purchased from the north, probably from the Ovambo, by the Auen, who cut the iron to shape, a flat head with two backward points at the sides on a short iron shaft which fits into the reed. These heads are tipped with poison. The Naron say they make the bone arrow-heads and the Auen the metal ones, but the Auen claim to make both kinds.

Poison is obtained from the grub or chrysalis of a small green beetle which frequents the bushes in early spring. The grubs come out in the summer, eat the leaves of the bushes and crawl down into the sand beneath, where they form cocoons. This happens about January or February. In both these stages they are used as poison, but the cocoon is preferred. It is dried in the sun and can then be kept some time and is easily transported. When wanted for use, the insect inside is rubbed to powder on a half tortoise-shell, then mixed with the juice obtained either from the spiked cucumber (*Citrullus caffer*) or from the "hakdoorn." They heat the cucumber root in the ashes, knock it on the ground, then wring out the liquid it contains. The bark of the "hakdoorn" is chewed, and the juice spat into the dish of poison. This juice is clear, bitter and sticky and adheres to the arrow point, on to which it is dabbed with a flattened stick after being mixed with the poison. The poisonous matter becomes very hard and dry and is apt to fly off into the eyes if the arrow is carelessly handled. Bushmen always warn one of this and say the eyes become much inflamed if even a tiny grain of dried poison gets into them. Any mixture left over is wound round a stick and carried with the arrows in the long bag. I presume it must be heated again if it is to be put on further arrow-heads. Sometimes the arrow-heads and poison are placed in a short leather quiver inside the long bag, but these are rare. The bow is either carried with one end in the bag, or loose over the shoulder, the string in front.

A knobkerrie or round-headed stick is carried by men on travel or seeking vegetable food. The lower end is pointed to act as a digging stick. It may be stuck in the long bag or else carried in the hand. Small bucks and hares are knocked over with it, and in minor quarrels it is the weapon of offence or defence.

Spears are sometimes used in hunting. The spear-head is purchased from the Ovambo in exchange for a long chain of eggshell beads. For the shaft they pierce the end of a stick, heat the back of the spear-head in the fire and insert it, binding the joint tightly with sinew. The spear is used for killing small game, or wild animals, such as leopards; but few Naron and Auen possess it.

Another implement, hardly to be called a spear, is used for catching spring hares, anteaters, etc., in their holes. Three or four long reeds are fastened together by bands of sinew, and a hook or horn is tied to one end. This is poked down the hole, generally a slanting one, and hooked into the animal's flesh, either to drag it out or to hold it tight while another man digs down to it. This unwieldy weapon may be seen leaning against a tree near a cluster of huts.

Shields are unknown among Naron and Auen. They say they know feathered arrows and sometimes make them, but I have seen none in use.

HUNTING AND TRAPPING.

There are no close seasons. Shooting is done all the year round, but trapping must cease in the rainy season owing to the action of the damp on the rope. The rope is home made from the fibre of the *Sanseviera zeylanica* which is shredded by means of a pointed stick, then rolled on the thigh into strands, which are twisted into rope, one end being held by the foot. Thicker and thinner cords are made according to the game to be trapped. Ostrich, paauw, etc., are snared by putting a bit of stick into a small tsama melon, tying one end of a rope to the stick and fixing the other end in a slip knot over the bushes round the melon, or some twigs placed around it. The bird swallows the fruit, thereby pulling the slip knot tight round its neck and is suffocated.

Small bucks and hares are caught in a trap made of a rope attached to a bent tree. First a circular fence of sticks about one foot in diameter and six inches high is made in a depression in the buck's path and covered with grass. In the middle a short, thick bit of wood stands upright. At one side the fence is broken by an arch formed by a bent twig from which a small stick dangles. A slip knot of rope is held open by the centre upright and this dangling bit of wood, the rest of the line is led round outside the fence, back through the arch and tied to a bent tree. Should the animal in passing step into the sling it jerks the cord off the end of the hanging pin, which keeps it from slipping; then the tree pulling upright tightens the slip knot round the leg of the victim, often pulling it right into the air.

As a rule Naron and Auen hunt alone, or a man and a boy together. They find a spoor, follow it, finally creeping up to the leeward side on hands and knees, using all possible cover, then gently raise themselves to shoot. The arrow only makes a tiny wound and falls down as the buck runs off. Sometimes the arrow point remains in the flesh, and the reed shaft only falls. The hunter recovers his property and leisurely takes up the spoor, looking carefully at the ground. He is forbidden to glance at the moon, lest the game run too far. Often he sleeps by the way, then comes up with the dying or dead buck, cuts it up, roasts and eats some and carries the rest home. If near the huts he may carry the whole buck home. Everybody comes round and has a taste, the hunter doling out the meat and of course keeping the skin, sinew, etc., for himself.

The Naron know how to make "biltong," that is, to dry strips of meat on the bushes to preserve them. But they do not often have occasion to do this nowadays, as not more game is shot than can be consumed in a very short time.

Hunting disguises are not used, but if a man sees a place where game comes to lick salt, he makes a hole in the ground for himself close by, piling the earth up in front and sticking green branches on top to deceive the buck. Here he lies in wait for a shot. Occasionally four men surround game in a pan, two stand to leeward ready to shoot, while two drive from windward, approaching from different quarters.

Dogs are not original Bushman possessions. They are given by Bechuanas, Klip Kaffirs or white men, for hunting jackals, leopards, lynx, etc. The skins so obtained are brought to the giver of the dog and bought by him at his own price for tobacco, or trade goods, chiefly the former. The animals are miserable looking underfed curs. They are sometimes used by the Naron to catch hares and small bucks for their larder, but never taken out to hunt larger game.

Guns have been known as foreign possessions for the last sixty years. A few Naron say they have shot with them while working for white men.

Snakes are caught with the long stick, like anteaters or spring hares. The man who pulls the snake out runs fast, dragging it after him, while others throw knobkerries and spears at it. This cannot be done in grass or the snake may escape.

After good rains the whole village decamps to the antheaps, in hope that the male white termites may fly out.

Someone digs a hole on one side of the heap, laying bare the opening to the underground homes. If the right moment has come, the winged males struggle up to the air, to start their flight, and fall into the hole, whence they are scooped into bags or eggshells. The sand is sifted out on a mat sieve made of reeds tied with home-made string. Then the termites are roasted on a fire close by and eaten without delay. They are considered a great dainty on account of their fat, in which a Bushman menu is often lacking, as only a few nuts of all the vegetable food contain fat, and most smaller bucks have little. Hence there is great rejoicing over a fat eland or a successful haul of termites. During my stay at Sandfontein no one dared touch an eland for fear of the police, but the whole village turned out promptly at the least possibility of the ants flying out, though often disappointed in their quest.

Burning the Grass.

Agriculture is unknown among the Naron. Burning the country at the end of the winter to make the bulbs come up better is the only step they have taken in this direction. Men may only burn in their own territory, to do so across the border, or to gather food where others have burnt, are great offences. In old days the captains are said to have regulated the burning. Now the thing is done haphazard, and generally passes as an accident.

A couple of Sandfontein Bushmen inherited a tobacco bed from their former Klip Kaffir masters two years ago, and have been endeavouring to keep it going, but with very poor results. On a neighbouring farm where the owner encourages and advises the Auen in his employ in growing tobacco, they are more successful, but they have no aptitude for gardening.

Neither Naron nor Auen possess cattle or goats. They depend on nature unaided to feed them. Lacking milk or soft food, meat broth is their only invalid diet. If they may not kill a buck, and have used up the supply of spring hares, etc. in their vicinity, when illness occurs, what are they to do? Cucumbers, hard berries and roast onions are not the food for a fever patient nor for a young child. It is difficult for us to imagine a life without milk, flour, fat and sugar, and when meat goes too, it leaves an enormous vacuum. The temptation to break the law and get a buck is almost irresistible, and as the penalty, if caught, is gaol, just as for stock theft, then the further temptation arises among those near settlers, to take the animal which can be much more easily killed.

TOBACCO.

All grown-up Bushmen smoke tobacco or dagga when they can get it. Most of their trade with other races, or service with them, is for obtaining smokes. In old days they used stone pipes, cut and bored by themselves out of a certain stone found in these parts. The pipe is simply a hollow tube, some three inches long, with a narrow and a wide end. The hollow shin-bones of small bucks are also used, but to-day empty cartridge cases are the staple article for smoking in.

Dagga is mixed with tobacco whenever obtainable. When taken in slight quantities it has no visible ill effects, but men are said to go wild and run off shouting after an excessive indulgence therein. The water-pipe is not unknown to the older men as used by their southern neighbours—they do not make or use it themselves.

Kaffir beer and all alcohol they enjoy when it is given them, but that is not often. They do not know how to make it themselves, nor do they seem to trade for it. Hence drunkenness is practically unknown among them, in spite of their appreciation of liquor. I gave a woman a dose of brandy to help her recover from snake bite. The cook-boy smelt at the cup enviously and told me that kind of medicine was very very "moi," one of the few Dutch words he knew. The woman tried hard next day to persuade me that she needed another dose.

GAMES.

Naron children have no playthings. The tiny ones amuse themselves with sticks and stones and grasshoppers. Boys soon make themselves a small bow and arrows to shoot little birds and reptiles. The arrows are either pointed sticks, or smaller bone-headed ones without poison. Both boys and girls go out with their elders collecting food, even the babies go, riding in their mother's kaross. The day is spent wandering in the open. In the evening the children run about near the huts or sit by the fire, till they feel sleepy and crawl on to the grass in the hut. No one sends them to bed.

However, they have some games, mostly played by the bigger girls with the younger children. I have seen a number of these.

I. *The Great Water Snake Game.*

One boy is the water snake. He crouches on knees and elbows close to a small heap of sand which represents the pool. Some ten yards off the other players sit flat on the ground, close behind one another; each one putting her legs on either side of the one before her, and locking her feet over the other's thighs, forming a chain with the biggest in front. They sway from side to side edging forwards as they do, meanwhile singing an old song of which some of the words are no longer understood. The first line means: "we are going to fetch water." The second is something about "very hot" or "very dry," but it is not in modern Naron speech. Now and then they interrupt their slow progress to dig up and eat in dumb show an imaginary water root. On reaching the "pool," the chain breaks up, all gather round the water and pretend to dip it out.

The "snake" from time to time flicks sand at them with hi finger, he is supposed to be squirting water. The others start back and scream, then gather once more round the "pool." At last the "snake" jumps up, seizes a victim and pretends to swallow it, which ends the game.

II. *The Elephant and Ostrich Game.*

Two players are the she-elephants coming to fetch water. Two others, the he-ostriches, are lying at the water. They jump up as the elephants approach, refuse to let them take water, kick and peck at them till they kill them and remain on guard at the water. All this is imitated without speaking or singing.

III. *The Ox Game.*

Three or four players are the oxen; they stand with their arms curved over their heads to represent horns, make big eyes and low. One player is the owner, another the claimant. These two dance about in front of the oxen, chanting: "My oxen they are, I refuse them; Thy oxen they are not, I refuse them; I say my oxen they are." Meanwhile the claimant gradually catches one ox after another and pulls it over to his side. When all are caught, the game is finished.

IV. *The Bartering Game.*

With a sort of sing-song patter of which the refrain is: "Give me goods," a couple sit on the ground opposite each other and imitate traders quarrelling over their goods and demanding more.

V. *A Sham Fight.*

Two lines of players stand about a dozen yards apart and pretend to shoot each other. They dodge about, avoiding the imaginary arrows, and gradually fall down feigning death, one after another, till only one is left. I saw this badly acted by girls; I fancy the boys would do it better. There was no singing with this game.

VI. *Getting Married.*

Two young girls go off in dance step and hide behind a bush; these are the brides. Two older girls with sticks over their shoulders follow their spoor, seize them and drag them away, these are the bridegrooms. The brides scream and struggle, whereupon two other players rush up, shake their fists at the grooms and try to release the brides. These are the brides' mothers. The bridegrooms push the mothers aside and walk off dragging the brides along by one arm. The other arm the young girls throw over their heads, pretending to weep. When they have gone far enough to demonstrate a successful capture, the game ceases. There is no singing in this game.

VII. *Ball Games.*

These are almost dances carried out by women and girls alone. Even grandmothers take part. I have seen three games, but there is little difference between them. The players stand in a line clapping their hands and singing a wordless tune, as they do in dancing. One player dances about opposite the others with a tsama melon or other convenient round object in her hand. At the end of the tune she throws the ball to the player at the right hand of the line, who dances out to catch it, and herself dances back to the left end, where she starts singing and clapping. The next player does the same. The game goes on till all have had several turns. Clever players throw the ball under the thigh. In one game two players stand opposite the line. The front player throws to the second, as she rejoins the chorus, while the second takes her place, and a third dances out to the second's place. The tunes and steps are very similar in all the games.

VIII. *The War Game.*

Young men and boys have games too. The favourite is called as above. Two players, or two lines of players half kneel, half sit on the ground opposite each other; they strike their breasts, then stretch out their hands to their opponents or touch the ground in between them, or pretend to throw something away. Meanwhile they keep up a queer noise, half hissing and half groaning and their faces express great contempt for the adversary. There seems little point to the game and no end save exhaustion; but the players enjoy it greatly and show much vivacity in it. I think it may originally have been the imitation of some animal fighting.

IX. *Throwing Sticks.*

This is a man's amusement, even middle-aged men join in. Each player gets a straight but pliable stick about a yard long, peels it and pares the ends to points. All run in turn to a rise in the ground, and throw the stick down in such a manner as to make it jump up and fly on. Each strives to make his stick go farthest. Then all pick up their sticks and start back again from the other side, continuing till they are tired.

MUSIC AND SINGING.

Young lads are very fond of playing a musical instrument, a monochord, copied from the Bechuana. It is a sort of wooden trough, along which a sinew is fastened, being attached at one end to a wooden peg on the raised side, at the other tied at the bottom of the groove. A tin can stuck over this end acts as sounding board. The string is played on with a tiny bow, which is generally moistened at the lips before use. The players produce a pleasant note or two, using a finger on the string to regulate the sound. They have no regular melodies.

The bow itself is no longer in use as a musical instrument, but is known to the older men. Of the instruments depicted in Stow's *Native Races of South Africa*, on p. 108, they knew all, but only identified Nos. 4, 5 and 7, namely, the bows with a tortoise-shell and a gourd sounding board, and the bow with the string tied in the middle, as having been made and used by their fathers. The rest they had seen among their southern and eastern neighbours. No. 6, they said, represented a number of single bows, which those engaged in a dance had laid down; one man would play on them with a stick. This they had seen in their youth.

The Auens also remembered a skin being tied over a pot to make a drum for big festivities.

All Bushmen sing, but their tunes are not easy for a European to distinguish, much less write down. They sing very high and never seem to hit the same note twice, though the tune remains the same. That is to say, they all go up together, but not from or to the same note, and all go down together, each hitting any note they please. The dance tunes are sung without words, the game songs still have words, but partly obsolete ones. I have obtained gramophone records of most of these and of one song unconnected with dancing, which seems to be a lullaby. It occurs in a scrap of folklore. The girls were very fond of this tune, and sang it on many occasions.

The time is perfect but no two in a chorus seem to hit the same note, though the general burden of the tune is kept up. Each dance has its own vocal accompaniment, but the general impression is so similar that one needs some experience to distinguish between them. Only the tunes sung at the initiation dances sound different. They are slow and solemn.

DANCING.

The ordinary dances have a social character. On any fine windless night after a good supper the girls begin clapping their hands and singing, standing near the huts. Soon a couple of youths turn up and start dancing round in front of them. Then more join, older men and women take part, till the whole crowd, save a few grandfathers, are singing or dancing. The men stamp round in a circle in time with the tune. In some dances a woman occasionally leaves the line of singers and dances round beside some man, who pays her attention in gesture, either holding a reed over her shoulders, or holding his arms out behind her, without touching her. The woman dances steadily round the circle without responding to the gestures, then returns to her place in the chorus. In other dances the men dance round alone, then approach the line of singers, holding out their arms. The courting motive is clear, though not indecently expressed in the social dances.

GIRLS' INITIATION CEREMONY.

When a girl reaches maturity, the eland-bull dance is held in her honour. All men and boys leave the village, save two grandfathers, who tie elands' horns, or wooden imitations thereof, to their heads and wait in the bushes. Some of the women stand in line singing and clapping, the girl is brought from her special hut, where she is kept during this period, and sits or lies by them. Other women circle round before them, lifting their karosses and petticoats to one side and exposing their buttocks, which they waggle from side to side. They have a particular slow, swaying step for this dance.

Then the two "bulls" stamp up and join the line, holding their karosses well pulled down over their shoulders. They have a jogging step and a hunched-up appearance. Sometimes they head the line, sometimes they are in the middle of it. The dancers make a circle or a figure of eight. The song accompanying it is full and low in tune, but without words.

The dance as I saw it was kept in moderation, but it might easily be very indecent, probably would be so among quite wild clans. I noticed that the older women showed no shyness about the performance, the younger ones, particularly those who had been with white people, contented themselves with places in the band.

This dance is held every night until the girl's period has passed. By day she is kept in the hut tended by women only; no men may come near her. The Auen hold this dance in the same manner. The Nusan recognized the tune. A similar ceremony takes place among them, a man with a bird's beak on his head taking the "eland-bull's" place.

BOYS' INITIATION CEREMONY.

When boys have learned to shoot and killed two or three head of big game, they go through an initiation ceremony. Ten or twelve of them are taken into the bush by medicine men and other old men and spend a month of hardship there. Their food consists of a few roots and berries on to which the medicine men sprinkle "medicine," that is powdered bark. The treatment they receive is very hard, the weaklings die. No woman may come near the camp. Every night they dance. All gather in a circle, clap their hands and sing a weird, solemn tune with the refrain of "honk a honk." Then they stamp round in a circle waving their arms to another phase of the melody (no words are used); then they stand still and sing the first part again and so on. I have seen this dance also.

The sound of the tunes used in these two initiation dances leads me to believe that they are the remains of religious ceremonies, of which the meaning is no longer clear to themselves. The men's function in particular might well have been an assembly for prayer followed by a dance.

On one of the nights of the |gi dance (the men's dance), a supernatural being called Hiſe approaches the dancers, circles round them and is driven away by the medicine men. The older men had seen this being. One said it was like a woman in appearance, another that it was not a person at all, but a creature about three feet high with a flat head, red eyes underneath the head, a black body, wings and claws. Some old Auens said two beings came, male and female, looking like lions, but walking upright. They were followed by children like baboons. The male came first and called the others, they danced round and vanished to the east.

Apparently medicine men of different times and places got up different bogies. Latterly their invention seems to have failed, for the middle-aged men told me Hiſe came to the dance, but only the medicine men saw her and drove her away.

On some day during this month all the boys are cut between the eyebrows, and, amongst the Auen, also on the back. There does not seem to be any ceremony attached to the act of cutting.

Besides the |gi dance, which one man called a dance to Hiſe, the ostrich dance is often performed during this month. Some half-dozen men stand in a circle. Two of them dance up to each other with an action copied from the birds, one ducks down, the other passes his leg over him, then ducks in turn, for the former to pass his leg over. They do this several times, then one player retires and another takes his place. The rest are stamping about in their places and singing a deep grunting song, rather like the "honk a honk" of the |gi dance.

Long ago they played another game as well. Two men danced up to each other, bumped their bodies together and retired, singing meanwhile: "||garo |na, Hiſe |na, !uku, *Ostrich stomach, Hiſe's stomach, hu.*"

At the |gi dance, the men often wear ostrich feathers, or the head and beak of the black and white stork as head ornaments. Otherwise they don't dress up. Anyone owning dancing rattles wears them, as at the ordinary dances. These are made of big cocoons, about one and a half inches long, pierced at either end and threaded on sinew. The chain thus formed is wound round the leg and the dried grubs in the cocoons rattle at each step.

RELIGIOUS BELIEFS.

Enquiries into the nature of Hiſe or Hiyeſa, as the Naron often say, led to the disclosure of a wonderful muddle of religious ideas. The people at Sandfontein are already in a transition stage— new and old beliefs are prevalent among them, and those latest acquired are most readily produced to strangers.

First the men from thirty to fifty years old said Hiſe was !khuba or !χuba, which my Klip Kaffir interpreter translated as *God* and then as *Heaven*, that is to say *the sky*. " !khub" is the Nama word for *master* or *lord*, and has been used by some missionaries to designate the Saviour. The young Naron were vague as to !khuba's nature, some said he was the sky, some that he dwelt in the sky; they prayed to him to let them live long and make them well when ill. When I asked the really old men, they replied that Bushmen were ignorant of him. "Missis" could read and write, "Missis" must know about !khuba and not ask Bushmen about him. To my enquiry, "Who told you about !khuba?" they replied, "The Namas," who used some decades ago to come down for hunting trips and stay for months together using the Bushmen as servants.

A very old man, a former medicine man's assistant, told me the first medicine man he had known as a lad had never mentioned !khuba and only "worked" with Hiſe, but when that generation was dead, the next lot spoke of !khuba and "worked" with him.

The women, who when young had been stolen and held as slaves by the Nama chiefs, were very fluent on the subject of !khuba, the others had evidently picked up the word without attaching any clear meaning to it, beyond that it was some sort of deity and it was "good to pray to it."

The old men told me later that Hiſe lived in the east. From the name it might be the spirit of the bush as "hi" means *tree* or *bush*. This being is evidently much the same as Heitsi Eibib, the Hottentot hero or divinity. "Hei" is Nama for *bush, tree.* "Eibib" means *the first.*

The Naron say, in olden times the trees were people, and the animals were people, and one day Hiſe bade them be animals and trees. Then he called the first captains of the white men and of the black men and said, "Take the cattle, take the goats and live by them." And to the first captain of the Bushmen he said, "Take the bucks and live by them, take the rope and make traps and hunt and live in the bush."

A few men mentioned Huwu or Huwuba as well, said he was Hiſeba's brother, they were two, but Huwu was the captain of the men in the north, the Makoba and others. They did not know much about him. One man called him the "captain" of the white men.

Both Naron and Auen also spoke of ||gaũwa. The Klip Kaffir promptly translated "Satan." But to my repeated enquiries among the Bushmen themselves, as to what ||gaũwa was, they all replied, "A person who has died." The men said: "All people who die become ||gaũwa and the medicine men can see them." The women said: "Only men who have been cut between the eyebrows become ||gaũwa and only such see them, though women sometimes hear them." They evidently mean ghosts, and have much the same vague idea of them as European peasants have. The ghosts walk at night and people are afraid of them, but do not expect real harm from them. If seen, the apparitions resemble people.

The wind is called ||gaũwa when it is strong and howls. Some individuals seemed to believe in a supreme ||gaũwa, a being who lives in the east near Hiſe, to whose house the ghosts repair by day. They said he was Hiſe's younger brother. Others said ||gaũwa was Hiſe. They evidently connect no ideas of good or bad qualities with either of these beings and do not seem to pray to them.

I think the transformation of ||gaũwa *a ghost* into a deity is the effect of intercourse with the Hottentots. Among the Kung ||gaũwa means *dream, spirit,* as well as *ghost.*

The moon is still worshipped among them, but they are very shy of admitting it. A medicine man and a woman sit on the ground together, hold their hands out, palm upwards to the new moon, and say, "Give us rain that we may live." A couple who still do it live at Sandfontein.

Their fathers used also to pray to certain stars, particularly to the morning star and the southern cross, which they call the "fire shoe." But these prayers are memories of long ago, whereas the moon worship is continued to-day by young as well as old.

The moon is connected with life and death in their minds. They have a version of the "Moon and Hare" tale common to all Bushmen and Hottentot races.

The Moon said: "People shall die and come back again as I die and come back again." But the Hare contradicted him and said: "They shall die and stay dead and not come back again." Then the Moon became angry and took his axe and hit the Hare on the mouth, cleaving it.

The Naron give the moon a masculine ending, the sun a feminine one. The moon is an old man, the sun a young girl, they are husband and wife. First the moon pursues the sun across the sky, later the sun follows the moon. They go down to their houses below the horizon in the west; then fly back at night across the earth to their houses in the east far away near Khama's country, which is evidently for them about the end of the earth. They can be heard passing but are not seen.

The Naron give Hiſe both masculine and feminine endings. The Auen have no such endings, but, as mentioned before, they tell of Hiſe appearing in both male and female form at their dances.

I think myself that the moon worship is their oldest religion. It is shared by all Bushmen and Hottentot tribes known as yet. It penetrates into modern ideas, for most of them think, as the moon is in the sky and the God (!χuba) the white men and Namas speak of is in the sky, that God is the moon.

The whole initiation ceremony for boys with the cuts is foreign to the Southern Bushmen and Hottentots. I cannot help suspecting that this was borrowed from their Bantu neighbours, generations ago, and grafted on to their own beliefs, at any rate coloured by their habits of thought.

The ceremony for the girls is a development of customs prevalent among the Hottentots, of which traces are found among the Southern Bushmen.

Medicine Men.

There are no priests save the medicine men and women, who
are also the doctors of the community. These do not dress or live
differently from the rest. No one would know them apart. They
do not seem to have much influence to-day. During the month of
the initiation ceremony one or two youths are taught their trade
by the old medicine men. At the next ceremony they return and
are taught more. They have a few roots and herbs as stock-in-
trade, but nowadays very little even of these.

The millipede, said to belong to Hiſe, is only touched by
medicine men, who used to dry it and use it powdered as
medicine.

When medicine men quarrel among themselves, they have
peculiar weapons for settling their differences, namely magic
arrows, or "grass arrows," as they call them. These are imitations
of real arrows about four or five inches long. The reed part is
made of grass, the bone arrow-head imitated in horn but only
with one sharp point, which is stuck into the grass. A miniature
horn bow goes with the arrows; all are put in a tiny leather quiver,
which can be hidden in their clothes or round bags. No poison is
used. A medicine man wishing to destroy another, comes up close
and shoots at the opponent's kaross with one of these arrows,
blunt end foremost. The missile falls harmlessly to the ground,
but the victim dies of the magic.

The Naron tell me they do not make or use "grass arrows"
much themselves, the !ginkwen and Auen use them more. Indeed,
the Auen seem to have far more medicine men than the Naron,
and are looked up to in "magic" matters.

The future is foretold by throwing a sort of dice, four pieces
of wood or leather, on to a kaross. Two of these are flat, two pointed;
the former are called the female, the latter the male dice. The ones
I saw were not marked in any way. Other men besides medicine
men may own and use them. The performance is very babyish:
they go on throwing until they get a favourable answer.

These dice, or divining sticks, are frequently found among
Northern and Central Bushmen, occasionally among those dwelling
on the southern borders of the Kalahari. The Colonial Bushmen
and those of Griqualand West do not know them. I think they
are decidedly adopted from the Bechuana, or other Bantu tribes,

as the frequency of their use coincides with the amount to which any tribe has been exposed to Bantu influence.

The way the Naron handle them shows they do not know much about them.

MEDICINE.

In curing a patient, medicine men and women work together, and sometimes have others to help.

One morning I heard dreadful cries and groans in the kitchen, and went out to see who was hurt. A man was ill and they were curing him. The sufferer sat against the wall, silent and doleful. Another man lay face down on the floor groaning. Then he got up, knelt by the patient and massaged him, assisted by a second man and two women, all chanting and groaning.

By and by one of the workers was supported to the open, where he stood groaning and screaming for some minutes, then appeared to throw something away, became quiet and resumed work. This went on for some hours; then the patient was better and walking about. I do not think he was very ill to begin with. Massage, perspiration and suggestion seem to be the means used. The medicine men are supposed to draw out the evil and throw it away.

When Naron have bad dreams, they put a bit of burning charcoal on the ground and pour water on it, then the bad dream flies away with the steam.

When a man is ill and Hiʃe sends bad dreams, after the sun has risen he takes a burning stick, plants it in the ground between his knees, burns buchu and snuffs it and recovers.

All have great faith in European remedies. Even the medicine men come to any white person for help if ill.

HEALTH.

They suffer most from heavy feverish colds every rainy season. Malaria crops up if there is sufficient rain to breed out mosquitoes, about once in five years, I should say. It carries off many victims. The "old" men used to cure it with the bark of some tree growing near Rietfontein, but the present generation have lost the secret.

They have no antidotes for poison, either that of their arrows or snake bite. The latter they try to cure by tying the snake skin round the limb. For burns and sores, buchu and similar herbs are rubbed on.

On the whole they seem healthy, as long as they keep to their own clothes and surroundings. European costumes and houses have a bad effect. They die in gaol like flies, chiefly, I believe, owing to the stone floors and the confinement. Being used to walk from five to ten miles a day and sit and lie in hot sand, they cannot stand the changed circumstances, however kindly treated by the gaol authorities. Magistrates should remember this in imposing sentences and rather give corporal punishment than a long term of confinement.

Motherhood.

The hardihood brought about by their free life shows itself in the women when motherhood approaches. They go out collecting food and wood till the last moment, walking as far as the rest. Births take place in the open, as often as at the huts. A little soft grass is collected wherever the event may befall, and any old woman or women present give their assistance. The mother sits during labour and is roughly massaged. She lies on her side during the act of birth, which is generally not prolonged.

The umbilical cord is not tied, just cut with a knife. A plaster of mud and leaves is put on the baby's stomach, if there is much bleeding. The child is wiped off with soft grass and put into the mother's kaross, then the latter gets up and continues her ordinary avocations, beginning by walking home, if she is at a distance. Her friends say, "Now you can eat nasty food again," meaning you can eat anything, which shows that daintiness is allowed before the birth.

Occasionally harder births occur, then the woman may lie quiet for a couple of days, if she pulls through; but a really difficult case means the death of both mother and child, as no method of helping save massage is understood by them. Should the child live and the mother die, some other woman may try to suckle it with her own, I am told, but more often the baby is buried with the mother, especially among the wilder clans.

Twins are rare. A group of women laughed at the idea that two babies could be born at once, but a middle-aged man remembered the birth of a twin boy and girl at a distance. Both children had been reared to adolescence, then the boy died.

After the birth there is often a squabble about the name between the husband's people and the wife's people, if both are present. The grandfather or grandmother will get the child named after him or her. Whichever party is in force generally succeeds. Should there be more children, when these names are used up, some uncle's or aunt's name is taken.

The children walk early, at about ten months; but long after a youngster can toddle, it still must ride in the kaross on the food-gathering expeditions. Some other woman or girl will often help with a young baby, but the bigger and heavier a child gets, the more it is left to its own mother. Till the youngster is weaned at three or four years it is her constant companion, coming for a drink every half-hour if it pleases, and giving her an additional burden to carry wherever she goes. Sometimes a father will put a big toddler on his shoulder for a bit. Otherwise the mother has no help.

Though children begin sampling all kinds of food as soon as they have teeth, they could not do without mothers' milk much sooner; a one-year-old or two-year-old can stand a taste of cucumber or a few berries, but would die of indigestion, if it had to eat enough of them to satisfy its hunger. This the mothers know, and feel also the impracticability of providing for two children of different ages but both needing the shelter of their kaross, and to be carried on marches. The Naron and Auen women therefore are determined not to have another child to rear till the first is able to do without their milk and care, say about four years old. Preventives being unknown to them, they "throw away" any baby born too soon, sometimes one, sometimes two, between the children they rear.

The men do not like this, they beat the women and say, "Do not throw it away" (so a woman told me), but the women take care that such a birth takes place in the bush, far away from home. When their time is at hand, they slip off with an old woman to a lonely spot, and try to force on the birth by massage. The child is sometimes still-born, but whether alive or not, it is at once buried by the old woman. That, in their phraseology, is not "killing" the child, but "throwing it away," or "leaving" it.

In consequence of this practice they do not rear large families. One or two middle-aged women counted up five children they had reared; the others are never mentioned. Their eldest children were already married, the youngest still quite small. But on an average the women do not rear more than three children.

In selecting which shall live they evidently go merely by the convenient time, not by the health of the infant, for I have seen several people with physical defects dating from birth.

FAMILY LIFE.

All Bushmen are very fond of their children. The child the Naron or Auen mother does undertake to rear receives her love and care without stint, and if it dies she still counts it among her children after the manner of Wordsworth's little maid.

Babies and young children are spoilt. Correction is rarely used, the mother is their slave. When finally dispossessed by a new arrival, the youngsters go out with other children, trailing after the women or bigger girls. Soon the boys go off alone, or walk and sit near the men, though not amongst them.

On journeys both parents often go together with the younger children, but for the daily collecting trips, one sees a group of women and little ones start off in one direction, single file of course, then some men in another, then four or five boys together, then girls, little and big, then more men and so on. In the afternoon the parties collect again at the huts, fires are started, the visiting begins and is kept up till late, supper being meanwhile prepared and eaten.

Only the owners sit in a hut, the visitors gather round the fire outside, women at one hut, men at another, the toddlers playing about everywhere, the bigger boys and girls by themselves. A woman often stays in her hut with her husband, even though members of the other sex are visiting; a man may stay with his wife, though the guests are women, but that is not so usual; he generally prefers to go visiting himself. No woman sits beside a man, unless he is her husband, father, uncle or grandfather or some lad much younger than she is. A grown-up brother and sister may on no account sit together, and are not supposed to talk to each other, but that they certainly do at a safe distance. Mother-in-law and son-in-law are also supposed to keep away from each other.

As to morals, the women told me a girl may do as she pleases, but a married woman may not.

MARRIAGE.

Marriage is nominally by capture. The word "to marry" means also "to fetch" and "to catch." The women said, a man seizes a girl of another village, and takes her to his village, and thereby she is married, whether she likes it or not. He comes with an older man just to pay a visit and sits chatting without mentioning his purpose. They look out for a good opportunity and carry the girl off. The bridegroom keeps watch on his bride at first, till she settles down. Later, when a child is expected, the young people come on a long visit to the girl's home, indeed, they may stay a couple of years there, and will always revisit it from time to time.

That is the theory—the practice no longer quite fits it. Talk about the marriage mostly precedes the capture. The mother thinks it proper to make a fuss, but if her objections are only for show, the men take no part in the matter, and the girl is led away, probably quite willingly, though etiquette demands some coyness.

If, however, the mother really objects, thinks her daughter too young, or does not like the suitor, she rouses the men to action, and the would-be bridegroom and his friend have to depart. An example of this occurred during my stay at Sandfontein.

One day, the Bushmen had collected in front of the house to give exhibitions of dancing for the purpose of photography. At mid-day we made a short interval. On coming out again, we found that all the men had gone; and were told that the huts were on fire and they had gone to put it out. We could see no sign of smoke or fire in the direction of the huts, and by and by some of the men began to trickle back, said it had been a bush fire, no huts were in danger.

Later, when I was alone with the natives, I was told what had occurred. One of the women had been at the huts with her young daughter and two Auen men from the north had turned up and tried to carry off the girl as wife for one of them. The mother lighted a fire to summon her men to her assistance. They arrived in time, and after a verbal quarrel, the would-be wife-stealer retired.

In old days much fighting was caused by attempted captures, now fear of the white man tames the affairs down.

Some girls marry very young, before they have reached the age of puberty. Others are unmarried at seventeen or eighteen.

I should say all were "fetched" before they were twenty. Youths seem to marry at about eighteen to twenty-one.

The rule that the bride must be from another village and that the young couple settle at the man's home is not strictly observed. At Sandfontein about half the married men were from other parts and had settled at their wives' home. In a few cases both were of one village. Apparently only the marriage of brother and sister is absolutely forbidden. Monogamy is the rule, but a second wife is not considered wrong among the Naron. Whether in such a case the women share a hut, or each builds herself one, depends on how they get on. I was told that it is better for a man to marry the younger sister of his first wife, if he wants a second, then they would not quarrel. One man attempted to get a second wife while I was there, but the girl's mother would not hear of it, and I was told his own wife did not want it either. The event did not come off.

A man having married, must make his wife presents. He gives her a full woman's kaross, other pieces of clothing and bead ornaments, which he gets by barter. When he visits the bride's parents after marriage he brings some gifts.

The constancy of the people varies. One sees couples who have grown old together, on the other hand one hears of cases of desertion on either side. If there are no children no one worries about it. If there are youngsters, the relations try to bring the parents to reason.

The children belong to the father. An unweaned child must go with the mother, in case of a separation, but the father can claim it later if he likes. People who have separated are not ostracized. Both parties generally marry again. If a man catches his wife misconducting herself, he tries to kill the other man, and beats his wife, but does not generally drive her away if she has children.

Widows often return to their own village. They mostly marry again, when young enough. The second husband is responsible for his wife's children. If a widow does not re-marry, her husband's brother is expected to help with the children. Old folks take a great interest in their grandchildren and often adopt one which has been weaned. There is no lack of family affection.

DEATH.

When death occurs, the body is tied with rope for purposes of transport, the knees being bent up against the chest, the position in which Bushmen always sleep. The same day a deep hole is dug where the soil is not hard; two or three men carry the body thither and lower it down by the ropes so that it lies on the left side facing the east. Why this position is customary they do not know. The dead are buried in their clothes, and all their possessions are placed in the grave, or if too long, as a bow or spear, hung on a bush close by. Then the grave is filled in, and bushes or stones are thrown on top to keep animals off.

All the village is present and the women weep. Next day a near relative burns buchu on the grave and says, "Tabete," *Good-bye*. Then all move to another locality and leave that spot for a couple of years.

In cases of haste or difficulty less ceremony is used. Bodies have been found buried in all positions and sometimes burial is impossible. When drought and scarcity force the people to a long, hurried march, some old man or woman may be too feeble to go with them. They make a screen of bushes all round the old person, provide a good supply of firewood and a little food and water if possible, and go. Should game and water be found within a couple of days' march, some young fellow is sent hurrying back with supplies. Otherwise they do not come near the place again, knowing that the end must have come and hyenas seized the remains. Anyone who falls out and dies on such a forced march will have to go unburied too.

I did not find that they were more afraid of the ghosts of the unburied dead than of those properly laid to rest, nor did they share the Klip Kaffir idea of "good deaths," i.e. deaths in a fight or an accident, and "bad deaths," i.e. deaths after a long, painful illness.

After the funeral there are no further mourning rites.

PUBLIC LIFE.

No questions of inheritance arise as no man has more property than is buried with him. Serious disputes among members of a village seem infrequent. They do not appeal to law, nor do they seem to have referred quarrels or cases of wrong-doing to their chiefs when such existed. Self-help appears to have been the rule, though fear of the white man makes it difficult to find out what really happens.

Saul, a Klip Kaffir constable, told me of one act of private vengeance, carried out by the father of a Bushman lad, ||eiseb, whom he had adopted. This man, an Auen, had a good deal of tobacco, most of which he hid in a tree. Returning later he found the tobacco gone, and human footprints round the tree. He followed the spoor to one of a cluster of huts near Habakobis, and saw a Bushman sitting at the fire cutting the stolen tobacco. ||eiseb's father had only a spear with him, but he darted up and stabbed the thief to death. The man's wife, intervening, was also stabbed. Then the assailant tried to escape, but was shot in the side by a poisoned arrow from the group round the next fire. He reached his home where he was arrested by Saul two days later, but died of the poison at Kwachanei police station.

A man who finds an ostrich nest with one or two eggs, sticks his arrow in the ground close by, as a sign of ownership, and waits till the tale of eggs is complete before carrying them off. Should another man take the marked eggs, the first finder follows the spoor to the thief's hut and demands them back. If they are given up, there is no fighting, but the thief does not escape reproaches for wrong-doing, especially from the neighbours of the finder. What happens if the eggs are refused is left to the imagination.

CHIEFTAINSHIP.

Both Naron and Auen had chiefs when the old men were young. The middle-aged men just remember them. One old man I met was the son of a former chief, an Auen, who settled and married among the Naron, then returned to the Auen and led them to victory over the Naron, and was finally accepted as chief by a section of the latter. Whenever his son, |kukurib, called Hartebeest by white men, is speaking Dutch, which the others do not understand, he asserts that he is now chief, but when speaking Bushman he never ventures to claim this, but chimes in with the rest, that there are no chiefs nowadays. I think he tried to rule after his father's death, but, on his people, under his leadership, being defeated by the Klip Kaffirs, he lost authority. His having often been absent working for white men may have contributed to this. Certainly he has no authority now save among his own family.

It was difficult to find out exactly what a chief's powers were.

They seem to have directed the movement of their people from place to place, to have ordered the burning of the veld, and in particular to have led in war. Fights were frequent both between the opposing Bushman tribes, Naron and Auen, and against other natives who were gradually encroaching from all sides, but the extent of each campaign was small.

Chieftainship is said to have been hereditary, but seems also to have depended on the personality of the successor. The chiefs did not dress or live differently from the others. Naron chiefs mostly had two wives.

It is impossible to discover what number of people each chief ruled over, Bushman arithmetic does not go so far. My own guess is that thirty to fifty families might acknowledge one man's authority, sometimes living all together round him, sometimes splitting up into tiny groups. There does not seem to have been any overlord or paramount chief among either tribe.

Leadership seems to have been an undefined and personal thing. The word used for the office is identical with the Nama word. Among Southern Bushmen there were no chiefs and they have no name for chieftainship.

There are no class distinctions among Naron and Auen, nor, excepting the medicine men, are there any trades. Some women are more clever and industrious in making beads than others, some men handier at twisting rope and boring pipes, but all know how these things are done, and none devote their life to them. Even the medicine men live as the rest do, getting a few presents for their occasional services.

TRADE.

Trade is limited to barter. This goes on perpetually between the members of one village, a little tobacco given for berries and roots, and so on. Visits to other villages and tribes to exchange goods are frequent.

The Naron are famous for making good skin garments and bags. These are exchanged with the Auen for metal pots, spearheads, knives, trade beads, etc., which the latter obtain from the north, and for wooden plates and spoons made by themselves. Ostrich eggshell beads are bartered by all tribes, but the Koon, a tribe to the south, are known to make them especially well, and their beads are always in demand. The Bantu races are good customers for beads. In dealing with white men and Bechuana, skins, chiefly jackal, lynx and leopard are given for tobacco, dagga or trade goods. The Klip Kaffirs and Bechuana also buy wild fruit and honey, generally for tobacco.

Bushmen are easily cheated, as they have little idea of values. They have no money nor any equivalent for it. Among themselves they may have a working rate of exchange for various goods, but the value of their possessions or services to a white man is beyond them. They often ask a ridiculous price, either far too high or far too low. They give a bead ornament that must represent weeks of work for a cheap knife, and then demand the same for a pipe stick, that has taken them an hour to burn. They will walk thirty miles carrying a fair load half-way for a handful of tobacco and a little mealie-meal, then want as much for getting a few buckets of water from the well at five minutes' distance. If refused, they take less of course.

ARITHMETIC.

In counting, they only use the numerals one and two *quite freely*. Three they sometimes use, taking the Nama word for it. If asked to count they go on up to ten, some using Nama words, and others saying "hand" and "two hands" for five and ten, and one or two vague numerals in between, corruptions of foreign words I fancy. For no two Bushmen count alike after three, nor does one man use the same sequence on two succeeding days. These higher numerals are evidently picked up from their neighbours by ear, and repeated without much consideration of their value, as a child of three will count in imitation of its seniors, varying the sequence of the numerals each time.

I asked a man: "How many steenbok skins do you take for a woman's kaross?" He said: "Two, and two, and two—so many," touching off his fingers as he spoke and finally holding up the six fingers to show. This man had glibly counted to ten that same morning. Anyone asked the number of children he has, will repeat each child's name, touching a finger to his lips, then hold up the number of fingers saying, "So many." Only if there are one or two do they answer directly without counting. If asked the length of a journey, they name the places at which they slept or will sleep, touching a finger to their lips for each, then hold up the fingers saying, "So many nights" (not days).

To express a large number they may say, "Two hands and a foot," but usually all numbers after the first few are "many," kei, and the greater the number the higher is their voice and the longer drawn-out the word. Likewise _!nu, *far*, can be made to express various distances by the inflection of the voice.

TIMES AND SEASONS.

The Naron distinguish three seasons: spring time, when the birds mate and the first flowers come, probably from August to October; summer, when it is hot and rain falls or is expected, about November till March; and winter, or the cold time, from April till July. When all seasons are past, a year is finished. The Auen have four seasons, winter, spring, the first rain time and the second big rain time.

They observe the sun enough to know that it makes a shorter path in winter than in summer, but apparently the stars foretell the coming of the seasons better. When the Pleiades (xwe:dzi) rise just before dawn, the cold is due; when they come before midnight, spring is at hand. Besides the Pleiades they have names for the Southern Cross (ɪɛ ||nare), Orion, the Milky Way (!nu ǂxɔni |wãba), and, I think, the Great Bear (|xɔnʃadʒi), which is just visible at Sandfontein. They know when each constellation will rise and set in the different seasons.

For shorter lengths of time, they go by the moon, but do not trouble themselves as to how many moons there are in a year or a season. A farmer told me that he engaged a Bushman by the month, using the Nama word which signifies moon and month. The Bushman turned up on the twenty-eighth day demanding his wages, and on being told the month was not up yet, was much aggrieved, asserting: "That moon is dead, Baas, it is a new moon." They observe the phases of the moon closely, but do not divide time into weeks. Yet when working for Europeans they quickly understand this division, and come regularly on the seventh day for tobacco, etc.

The Naron have no words for north and south. For east and west they say simply sunrise and sunset. Otherwise they distinguish points of the compass by the names of the tribes dwelling in each direction, viz. the Auen's country, the Auen's wind, for north, and the Tsaukwen's country, the Tsaukwen's wind, for north-east, and so on. The strong west gale has a special name, "wurri," by which it is also known among the Cape Bushmen. The word imitates the wind's whistling.

TRADITIONS.

Their history is bounded by the memory of the oldest men. Traditions are few, and little folklore is left.

They are the Bushmen of the road, the Ngami road, long known to travellers for its succession of water-holes. This is their pride, they have seen occasional white men from childhood and are more civilized than their neighbours right and left in regions where water is scanty. This makes them less valuable to the anthropologist, but as the wild Bushman is unapproachable, one must make the best of the half-tamed one.

According to the old men, there were neither Ovaherero nor Bechuana in their territory till they had reached middle age, though they had dealings with the latter along their eastern border. Klip Kaffirs have always dwelt among them, especially in the western part of their land; they traded with them and some-times worked for them. The Makoba near Ngami were known to them by hearsay, as bad people who eat Bushman children. The Nama did not live in their country, but used to come for hunting expeditions with waggons and guns, staying many months. They took Naron girls to live with them and made all the tribe do odd jobs for them. Still they shot much and were liberal with food, so that their coming was not disliked.

The Auen to the north and the Nusan to the south were hostile. Trespass and wife-stealing led to many fights with these. But the Bushmen to the east and north-east, the Tsaukwen, Tsorokwen and !giʒkwen were friendly. These all spoke similar dialects to the Naron, they could understand each other and recognize each other as k"am-ka-kwe *mouth's people*.

When the oldest men were lads, smallpox swept over the country. First the Bechuana had it, then the Bushmen took it, and finally the Klip Kaffirs and Nama caught it from them. Large numbers died. One man is badly pock-marked, and another, who had it as a baby, has been blind in one eye ever since.

At a later date a fever came, without spots, and carried off many victims. Several bad famine years are remembered some decades ago when numbers perished. All agree that there are fewer of their people to-day than in their youth.

As to traditional history they tell of no chiefs but those they remember. There is a legend shared by the Klip Kaffirs that these and the Naron both pulled at a rope (apparently for the possession of land). Then the captain cut the rope (between them) and said to the Bushmen: "Take your rope and go into the bush and trap game." And they did so, and the Klip Kaffirs remained (in possession of the land). This is evidently a variant of Hiſe's division of peoples. I give another variant later. This tale was told me as history.

ART.

At certain points along the ridge which divides the Auen and Naron there are rock engravings of patterns and animals. Some are exceedingly old, others less weather-worn. I have seen them at Babibabi about half an hour's walk from Mr van der Spuy's house, and have been told there are many at Tsachas not far from the watering place.

Neither Naron nor Auen knew anything about them. Only one or two had seen them and these were inclined to echo the Klip Kaffirs' prompt verdict that they were the work of ||gãũwa.

Certainly neither tribe knows anything about painting or chipping to-day. I doubt if the Naron ever practised these arts. They strike me as a very prosaic people, very different from the highly imaginative Southern Bushmen who were known to paint and engrave till within the last century. Moreover, living in the sand, they have little stone to work on.

The Auen, though to-day not very different from the Naron, have in their faces and bearing traces of a wilder, freer race, whom one would credit with more fancy. Whether their ancestors painted and carved stone long ago, or whether these traces of art were left by southern tribes who may formerly have occupied the territory, is an unanswerable question. Possibly the older chippings date from the period before the northern and southern languages developed from the parent stock.

CHARACTER.

I was much struck by the respect the Naron had for the Auen, particularly for those farther north, the "proper Makoko Bushmen," as my interpreter called them. On the other hand, the Auen had no great respect for the Naron, in spite of many of the latter being more civilized than themselves. The Naron are more timid and peaceable, the Auen hardier and bolder. But the southern tribes were certainly fiercer than either; they died fighting and even though overwhelmed by the Bantu tribes in the east, never expressed anything but hate and scorn of the "black man." They accused him of cowardice, they mocked at his large ears and feet, and caricatured these in their pictures. They regarded Hottentots as their equals, never as their masters; and either fought them or married them, as chance might ordain. Nor did they easily give in to the white man, often preferring death to servitude.

The Naron call the Hottentots "masters," and sometimes apply this term to Klip Kaffirs and Bechuana. They let themselves be tyrannized over with very little resistance. They are dreadfully afraid of the white man, particularly the policeman, who appears to them merely an arbitrary tyrant, as they do not understand the laws, and never know what they may be arrested for. They have no idea that the law can protect as well as oppress them, and the very young lads who enter the police force and wield immense power when far from the magistrate and without white witnesses, are not likely to teach them this fact. Half the convictions of Bushmen under the game laws would not take place, if the accused did not let themselves be frightened into owning to the police which of them shot the bucks, whose skins have been found near a group of huts. The white man would say, prove who shot it, and the police would be helpless. They take care not to warn the natives that anything they say will be used against them. When Bushmen appear in court they have no idea of what would be accepted as a defence or in mitigation of sentence, and the interpreting is mostly done by native constables who are anxious to please the white policemen they serve under and to "make a case." It will take a long time before it dawns on these primitive people that the laws are intended to be just to them as well as to others. Until that happens the wilder elements, which are certainly to be found among the northern tribes, Auen and Kung, will occasionally resort to self-help, i.e. the bow and poisoned arrow.

Towards a master who treats them decently Bushmen are faithful and honest. At Sandfontein there were no locks or bolts. My storeroom, with tobacco, sugar, and many other things they like, stood open day and night, but they never helped themselves. They would beg shamelessly, however, like the children they are.

Their child nature shows itself in many other ways. They do not worry. They see their race dwindling, their land being invaded right and left. Yet when the sun shines and food is plentiful, they eat and drink and are merry and dance all night. They never fret about what may happen. That I think is characteristic of all Bushmen.

Physical Appearance.

The inability of the northern and central tribes to defend their women from their stronger neighbours shows itself in the large admixture of black blood. Hottentot connections are more difficult to trace, but the darker colour, greater height, flowing muscles and broad faces found among the dwellers north of the Molopo, tell their own story. In between, one finds persons of slight stature and yellow tint, whose curious small faces remind one of the southern tribes. Some of the young men of typically Bushman appearance are more like girls. Their arms and legs are no bigger than those of a healthy European child of twelve, the faces are not particularly masculine, and when they sit at a fire wrapped in a kaross one is apt to take them for women, especially when they are wearing beads in their hair.

Capacity as Workmen.

Yet it is surprising what good work these effeminate-looking limbs can do. Both Naron and Auen can be trained to be fair farm hands, but only slowly, with great patience, and that the young farmer, struggling to make his fortune on the outskirts of civilization, rarely has. Older men, who have worked with them for years, prefer them to other natives, as being more biddable and more honest. But all say one must give them much time to learn, not merely their job, but habits of industry. When the master sees a man get restless, he must let him go, to wander about and look for wild food for a time, taking another in his stead. There is never any lack of hands on the land of any man who settles in Naron or Auen territory and is friendly to them. They consider him a protection against the police and always beg for a pass, as a sort of magic guard against arrest.

I travelled twice by donkey waggon alone with Bushmen, who did their work as well as the other natives of these parts, and went home alone with the waggon afterwards. Of course there are bad characters among them, but as a rule they are trustworthy to the man who wins their respect and keeps faith with them.

Few will be given the chance to survive and settle down as workmen. The change comes too rapidly to let them develop; when the man who works arrives, the hunter and food gatherer is doomed.

FOLKLORE.

The folklore of their fathers is being rapidly forgotten by the Naron. At first all denied any knowledge of "stories," but when I had learned enough Naron to translate from *Specimens of Bushman Folklore* to them, these reminded some old people of this or that tale they had heard in their youth. The young folk hardly knew any, and even the old folk did not remember all the stories. The Naron tell a story so badly, that I had to keep asking, which person does "he" refer to. Still I have made the translations as literal as possible; words in brackets are my additions.

The Moon and the Hare.
(First version by ǂnu ⁻kei.)

!õãʃa ‖nweba _kɔaʃa |k'abo k''ɛː. |eːʃ kwe _kuru_kurua, me ⁻maː.

"Kwe‖kwa ga ʃi ⁻‖oː tite," ta ⁻mi. Xaʃa ma, "Kwe‖kwa ga ⁻‖oː," taʃ ⁻mi.

Kam ʃɛ bɔːʃa, a ‖kau k''amʃa.

TRANSLATION.

The Hare doe threw (her) kaross at the Moon's face. In the fire singed it and gave it him.

"Men shall not die," he said. But she replied: "Men shall die," so she said.

Then he took an axe and split (her) mouth.

(Second version by |kukurib.)

!õãʃa _kɔaʃa |eːʃ kwe _daua, a ‖nweba |k'abo k''ɛː, a _dau k''ɛː. ‖nwem-di k''ɛːʃa _ǂnu _kɔaʃa i. ‖nweba k'xai, a ʃɛ _kɔaʃa, |nam me xuː, a |k'abo xuː.

!õãʃa ko ma, "K''au‖kwa |ɛba !kum-di kwe ‖gai kweʤi ⁻keiʃi ʃɛ, ⁻kei |kunku." ‖nweba ⁻‖kwi, "K''au kwe ⁻‖oː tite. K''au kwe |kanisa uːwa ha, a xanxaba ko |kwane ‖gai kweʃa ⁻maː, ⁻keinʃ ab⁻ai kwean ⁻kei, ⁻keiʤi kweʤi ⁻u, ‖gai kweʤi ⁻u, ⁻kei kwene."

TRANSLATION.

The Hare singed her kaross in the fire and threw it at the Moon's face, and burnt his face. The Moon's face is black from the kaross (allusion to the mountains in the moon). The Moon cried and caught the kaross and threw it away, flung it away.

The Hare said, "Of men that one who marries many women shall be killed." The Moon contradicted: "The man shall not die. The man has leave (? a letter), and he to each woman shall give children, so that they may bear many people, many men may bring forth, many women bring forth, many Bushmen."

(Third version.)

!õ̃ʃa ko ||nweba _kɔaʃa |k'abo k''ɛː, me _dau k''ɛː. ||nweba k''xai, a k''ɛːʃa ʃɛ, a au ⁻xuː, a |k'abo ⁻xuː.

"Kwe||kwa ga ⁻||oː," taʃ ⁻mi. Me ||nweba ⁻||k'wi, a ma, "Kwe||kwa ga k'wẽː," taʃ ⁻mi. Kam bɔːʃa ʃɛ, a ||kau k''amʃa. ʃi k''xai, a _kɔaʃa _kuru _kuru |eːʃ kwe, a |k'abo k''ɛːme. A !nɔxo k''ɛːme, ta ho ⁻kwa kuruʃi xuːd̨i iː.

|naʃ !õ̃ʃa ko ⁻||kxwi, a ko ma, "M ⁻||o: me," təme.

K''au kweba duːba |kũ, ⁻kei k'ãeaba ⧧aː, a tane me a, a !õ̃ʃa ⁻maː. A ||ẽi !nuʃ ⁻kwe, a k'ãeʃa ⁻maː ʃi.

ʃera _are tʃaʃa, _!kau_!kauʃ |kwa, a _ha _k'aː. A ʃi a ||ka ʃe, ⁻keiʃe _!kau_!kauʃe ma ||ka||ka teː, a |ni taxa iː au ⧧kaː ʃi, |ni ta tʃaʃ kwe |k'abo ⧧kã̈ ʃi; ʃi tʃaʃ kwe ⧧kãː. ʃi tʃaʃa !õ̃ʃa tane, a !nuʃ kwe ||ẽi, xam duːba |õ̃ _ha !nuʃ kwe.

Me kweba tane ha k''ɔxwane, a k''aeʃa maː ʃi !õ̃ʃa. ʃi ||kã ||kaia |gabe, a |xã̈ː, me ko !kaː.

"Ti hoʃa, m d̨a tʃe _haʔ" taʃ ko mi, ʃi _dana ⁻a. !õ̃ʃa !nuʃ kwe ʃi ⁻!nuː, a ko kːxai, "Tʃwa, tʃwa, tʃwa."

Kam ko kweba ||k'um, a ko ⁻kum, a ||gum ||nad̨i zi xumʃ kwe !kai !nɔxo, ʃi ||k'we iː. ⁻Keiʃi iː, "tʃe, tʃe, tʃe, tʃe! Duʃa _!kɔxo !kai ⁻teʔ" taʃ ⁻mi. a _||oː.

ʃi ||kuʃa, |kwaʃiʃa ʃe, a ma, "ʃi gwi ʃi," taʃ ⁻mi, "ʃi _!guwa ⁻||k'we. |niːʃa xaɔ na eiʃa _||oː," taʃ mi. "Oaxa ʃam ⧧kũ ʃi |eʃ kwe, na k''oː ʃi," taʃ ⁻mi, "⧧ku na." ʃera k''ɔ ʃi.

TRANSLATION.

The female Hare at the Moon's face threw her kaross and burnt his face. The Moon cried, took (it from) the face, and threw it away.

"People shall die," she said. But the Moon contradicted her and said: "People shall live." Then he took his axe and split (her) mouth. She cried and singed the kaross in the fire and threw (it) at (his) face. He wiped his face, for ashes hot things are.

Then the Hare cursed and said: "He shall die." So it is said.

A man killed an Eland and cut out the intestine and brought it and gave it to the Hare. (She) stayed in his hut, and he gave her the intestine.

Both went to the water with a waterroot and drank. She splashed it very much, washed the waterroot, and thus pushed it in, like this into the water-hole threw it; it fell into the water. Then the Hare carried water, and stayed at the hut with the Eland's body.

A man came carrying meat and gave the intestine to the Hare. She licked it, and rubbed fur with it and wiped, he watched.

"My wife, what are you doing?" he said, and ran away from her. The Hare stayed at home and cried: "Tshwa, tshwa, tshwa!"

When the man slept she listened, took a piece of stick and stuck it into the ground. She lay there (on the stick). Much she cried: "Tshe, tshe, tshe! What is sticking into me?" So she said, and died.

Her mother spoke: "Lift her up," she said, "she sleeps in death. Long ago is daughter dead," she said. "Bring her and roast her in the fire and eat her," she said, "when roasted."

The above tale was given me as a sequence, but I think parts must have been omitted. Probably the change of the Hare from a person to an animal was in the original and other details which would make the story less confusing. Questions did not help much. I could not find out whether the "man" simply means the Hare's husband, i.e. another Hare, or not.

The Wind and ||gãua.

≠aba kwemə e:, a !kũ. A tʃaram ga ||gãuaba ≠am |kwa !kũ. ||gãuaba i:, _Hi ʃeba i:, |kwimẽ, a ⁻|kʌm |kwəʃara u:wa _ha.

≠aba ||gãuaba u:wa _ha, a !kũ tama, _gwe, xumʃa _gwe, a !narim kwe ≠kã:, a |ni ta i: ⁻:xwe; a |gãdʒi ʃɛ:, a ⁻ta: kwe ʃi ⁻a: xu, a xam ko _ka: kwe ʃi _ka:.

Tʃɔ k″auba a m: tʃaraba ≠a:m |kwa !kũ. Tʃaraba ||gãuaba i:. ||gãuaba ⁻biri, "Ti ≠aʃa ⁻kuru, a ||na ko !kũ." Ta ⁻mi.

TRANSLATION.

The Wind is a man and goes out. As a bird ||gãuwa with the Wind goes. ||gãuwa and Hiʃe are one and have two names.

The Wind has ||gãuwa with him and walks no more, rises up, from the earth rises, into the sky goes and thus flies; and takes grass and throws it elsewhere, at a far off place it falls.

The Medicine man sees the bird walking with the Wind. The bird is ||gãuwa. ||gãuwa says, "I make the Wind and thus go!" So they say.

Division of the Earth.

||e:xaba ⁻mi, ||kuŋ ⁻≠aro kwena ko !gweba ⁻!xo:. Kwena k″am ka _hana, |hũ na _hana ha, gome ⁻i:, byri ⁻i:, gu: ⁻i:. Ka |hũ ko ʃɛ,

a |un |kwaː, a !xo !hum, a ma, kwe ||eːxaba !gwiʃ: |kwa ⁻|kwaː, "ʃa-tu !gwiba ʃɛ, na !num, na k″ɔː. !geiba !num, na |nouʃa !num, na k″ɔː, na ⁻kɔaʃa ⁻kuru, na ||keina _hã. Nere tire a ha a |xeːdʒi _hã; tuːʃa ⁻tuː, _kɔadʒi hã." Ta ⁻mi.

_!xu ||eːxaba. |hũba ko ⁻!xo, kweba ko ⁻!xo, ||eːxaba ko xau ⁻kum, a kwena bəri: "!geidʒi ⁻ʃɛ," a |hũ||kwa "gwedʒi ⁻ʃɛ."

Kwe ||eːxaba !gwiːʃa ʃɛ, tam ko _!xuba i a _|gɔra. Me ko kwe ||eːxaba ||neiʃ !oːkwe ko _haba.

Ko bəri ||kaie, "||ei tʃera ko _|kara ku; |ɛba gwedʒi |kwa ⁻|kwa, |ɛba !geidʒi |kwa ⁻|kwa, a ko !geidʒi ko !num."

"A ko me nabo kwe ||gaikweʃa, kweba !gwiʃa !num, a ko !geidʒi k″ɔː." _!xuba ko |hũba bəri, m tsa.

TRANSLATION.

The Captain said, the Old People (first people) should pull at a rope. Bushmen were there, white men were there, cows were there and sheep and goats. Then the white man took (hold) and pulled for them, and pulled (the rope) asunder and said, as the Bushman Captain divided the rope: "You take the rope and trap and eat. Trap steenbok and trap duiker and eat, and make karosses and sling them on. While I will wear clothes, when it rains will wear blankets." So he said.

!xuba was the Captain. The white man pulled, the Bushman pulled, the Captain cut (the rope) in two and said to the Bushman: "Take the bucks!" and to the white men: "Take the oxen!"

The Bushman Captain took the rope, as !xoba divided it. Then the Bushman Captain went away among the "tsama."

They said to each other: "Both live separate; one go with the cows, and the other go with the bucks and trap the bucks."

"The Bushman women shall gather food, the men shall make traps and eat bucks." This !xuba told the white man (in a dream) as he lay and slept.

The Elephant and the Children.

|kwã khara ||kaue ha. !nɔxoi a a !kwã xuːi. A !kwã xuːi ||kunʃa. Me !xoaba a te !gau khara a. Khara tẽ a !xoa !aba be, eisa teme a. Khara si !aba be a !nuː, ǂku !aba kwe.

Ga hem ko ||gã khara, ga hem ko ||k'wĩ. Khara ko ⁻k″xai, a ko ⁻maː,

"Kama he, kama he, kama he!
Tʃoxam ||kanaba i?
Eiʃe a |geː.
Xõ kʌm ||kanaba i eiʃa a |kum."

Two children (boy and girl) were waiting. They had been left behind. Their mother had left them behind (to get food). An Elephant stood near the two. The two got up and climbed up (him), thinking of mother. They climbed far up him on to the head (to look out).

They both tried to get down, but he refused (kept turning round). The two cried and sang:

> "*Kamma he, kamma he, kamma he!*
> What magic camelthorn tree is this?
> Mother is coming.
> Stand still, camelthorn, that from mother I may drink."

The song with which the story ends is still much sung by women and girls. The words are partly obsolete, but the narrator, the only woman who seemed to fully understand them, gave me the above meaning, and told the story in explanation. The song I took down with the phonograph.

Story-telling seems to be dying out before the advance of civilization.

The Paauw and the Ostrich.

(First version.)

ǂgau ⁻keiba, |garo ⁻keiba i:. Xaba ǂgau |kwaʤi tʃera ⁻|kũ a _k″ɔ:, a m |ɛba (|garo ⁻keiba) dəbi _ha, kum |kwaʤi ||aiʃ kwe k′ai:. Keim ǂnu a ⁻kum, a _tʃu:, n ǂkau a ⁻||xwa, a ma, "Xaba ǂxana te, ti |kwaʤi k″ɔ:."

A |kwaʤi tʃera _are _tʃa⁻ʃa, a _ha, a m |garoba k′ai, a k″a: |garo ⁻keiba. Keim ||na ǂnʌm ǂgouba _are. "Ma ʃãu nere tʃaʃa k″a," tam ǂgou ⁻keiba mi. |nai m k″a, a ʃu:ʤi ʃɛ, a !nɔxo, a xam |õãʤi !o:. |ni tem ba ⁻||kwe, _keim ko !o:. Keim xaba ʃu:ʤi k″o, a ǂi: me. Keim ʃu:ʤi ⁻oe, me ⁻k″xai, hiba ʃɛ, a |garon |nuk″em ⁻||kʌm. Ta ko hĩ kwene e.

The Paauw was there and the Ostrich. He, the Paauw, killed two children and ate them and saw the one (the Ostrich) come home, heard the children at home cry. When at night he (the Paauw) heard them he was angry, his heart was sore, he said, "He (the Ostrich) has deceived me, I have eaten children."

Two children (the Paauw's) fetched water and came and saw the Ostrich crying (as he lay), and (gave) to drink to the big Ostrich. Then the Paauw came to the water. "Give me, that I drink," so the Paauw said. Then he drank and fetched a pot and put it down and he put in bones. Like this he (the Ostrich) lay, while he (the Paauw) put them in. Then he carried the pot and dropped it. When the pot fell over, he cried out and took a stick and beat the Ostrich's legs. At that time they were people.

(Second version.)

Xaba |xana ma, "|kwaʤi ǂkũ tʃam k″ɔː." A hi |kwaʤi ǂkũ, tʃara k″ɔː.

Keim |ɛba ||aiʃ kwe ||ai a ⁻hã. |kwaʤi ⁻kei. |kwaʤi "ɛ, ɛ" təmi. |ɛba kum. "|kwaʤi _hana ha. _Dum ko |xana te na |kwaʤi ǂkũ, xaba k″ɔː," ta ⁻mi.

Keim tʃara tʃaʃa _hare, |kʌm a, a, ʃi k″aː. |ɛba (ǂgouba) k″aː, tʃaʃa k″aː, |ni taxa i ||k′we. |ɛba (|garoba) ma, "ʃo, na re k″a."

Xaba ||k′we, na ba ǂkã: k″a təme, ǂka: tʃa k″aː na. Keim ma demi, me |k″ai, a hiba ʃɛ, a ⁻||k″ʌm me, |ni kwe ⁻||k″ʌm me.

Tʃera ||kẽi ku, a ⁻hĩ ku, a ʃi me ||aiʃ kwe ǂkã:. Ma |ɛba ⁻tʃauaba ʃɛː, a ʃiː. Ko keim ⁻||wi, a ma, "|niʤa ⁻!nai" təme. Keim |niʤa ⁻!nai, a xumʃ kwe ǂkã:.

⁻Ta ko hītʃara kwetʃara a, |garoba kweba iː, ⁻ǂgouba kweba iː. Tʃara ⁻hĩ ku. |niːʃe koko ⁻iː iː. Wɛ: xuʤi ko kweʤi iː. Ko ⁻|kwixa aː.

TRANSLATION.

He (the Paauw) deceiving said: "The children roast for us two to eat." And they the children roasted and both ate.

Then one (the Paauw) at home stayed. The children were many. The children cried: "E, e!" He listened. "Children are here. Then he has deceived me and children roasted and eaten," he said.

Then both to the water went, being thirsty, that they might drink. One (the Paauw) drank, water drank, and thus lay (by the water). The other said: "Wait, that I may drink."

He lay still, and he (the Ostrich) went down to drink, went down to the water and drank. Then he (the Paauw) pushed him and he fell in, and a stick picked up and struck the other, like this struck him.

They ran after each other and he (the Paauw) raced and popped into his hole. But the other got a digging stick and came. Then he flew up and said: "Tie it here." While the other tied it, he went into the ground.

At that time they both were men, the Ostrich was a man, the Paauw was a man. Two they were. Like this it was. All things were men. It was in the beginning.

The Lion and the Hyena.

|nutʃwaʃa !gẽi ǂkuːʃa hiːm‿kwe |gẽː, a xam-di ||aiʃ kwe _haː. Ka xam ba m ‾ʃiː, a ma, "!kẽsis ko _ha," təme. |ɛba ma, ko ||kʌm, "bɔː, bɔː, bɔː," təme.

||xauba _karue |nutʃwaʃa, a xaba ||xau a ʃɛ, a _dau _tʃwaʃa. Si ko, "ŋ, ŋ, ŋ, ‾ta _dau, _toa _te," taʃ‾mi, a ko !xwe.

ǂgauba a |õǎʤi ʃɛ, a |name ʤi |nutʃwaʃa. Ko kam ||ẽxaba "futsek[1]" təme, a ko |õǎʤi ko ||gai kweʤi ʃɛ, a |kwa||kwa ma.

A kuwa |ni taxa !kuŋ, |ni taxa tʃaʃa _hã, a k″aaː; a !ka ‾u, a |niː ||ai kwe !kuŋ, a |õǎʤi xãũ. Ta ko ‾hĩ kwe ‾mi.

TRANSLATION.

The Hyena came carrying the steenbok's head on a stick to the Lion's house.

The Lion saw him come and said: "Come in nicely." So he said and blew up (the fire), "bo, bo, bo."

The spear was heated for the Hyena, and he (the Lion) took the spear, and burnt the (Hyena's) anus. "Ng, ng, ng. Don't burn (me), leave me alone," he cried, and ran away.

The Paauw picked up the (steenbok's) bones and threw them at the Hyena. Then the chief (the Lion) said: "Get out." The women fetched the bones and gave them to the children.

Like this (bunched up with pain) he (the Hyena) went along, like this to the water came and drank; and went off and late to the house came and gnawed the bones.

So the people say.

An Auen Folk Tale.
The Lion and the Hyena.

xam tʃ'u si ‾!kou ku ‾tsiː. xam ‾|ka au ‾ʒu o ‾!kha. ‾!kou u ku tʃi !ne. ‾ʒu _kɔa tʃi. ‾!kou o k'wi xam, "a ‾tsiː m ‾tʃ'u." xam ku ‾tsiː a !kou ‾tʃ'u.

"mihi ku ‾au a msi dama _!goːma o tsiː, mihi ku _|uːwa ha tsiː. mihi ku guːwə, a ku _|uːwə dzousi tsiː, si ku m. mihi ku guːwa, a ku _|uːwa msi a tsiː, ahi m."

Ha ku guː k'ɔː, ku _|uːwa xam |ni e. k'ɔː ‾khwi, ku ku ‾uːwa ɛam |ni. hai ri ǂki.

TRANSLATION.

To the Lion's hut the Hyena came. The Lion did not give the person to eat. The Hyena is a thing that bites. People fear the thing. The Hyena said to the Lion: "You come to my hut." The Lion came to the Hyena's hut.

---

[1] Dutch "voetzak."

(The Hyena said:) "I give food to the little child here, I put it into his mouth. I take some and put it into the women's mouths, that they may eat. I take some and put food into your mouth, for you to eat."

He took the pot and put it on the Lion's head. The pot was hot and burnt the Lion's head. He died.

GRAMMATICAL SKETCH.
NARON.
Orthography.

The Naron speak with their teeth almost or quite closed. In consequence it is difficult to distinguish vowels clearly. They are apt to run into one another. We find:

i, iː, y, ə, e, eː, ɛ, ɛː, a, aː, ʌ, ɔ, ɔː, o, oː, ɯ, u, uː;

and the diphthongs:

ei, ai, ao, aɔ, au, ou, ɔa and ua changing into wa, ue into we, and ui into wi.

All vowels and diphthongs can be nasalized.

Of labials we find m, b, w; b at the end of a word is pronounced p by some individuals—otherwise there is no p.

f and v only occur in imitations of sound, as of the wind. They are bilabial.

t and d are very frequent, likewise n and ŋ. n in the middle of a word often approaches a non-rolled r.

l does not occur. In foreign words it is replaced by r.

s and ʃ are very frequent; z and ʒ less so; generally the latter follow d.

j occurs in endings, probably as a contraction of a vowel.

h and x occur both alone and after gutturals. x varies in sound according to the vowel following, being formed forward before front vowels, at the back before back ones.

Of gutturals k is most frequent, g less so. Many Nama words with g have corresponding words in k in Naron. kh, k', and k'' also occur. This last is a strong plosive croak. We find kx, k'x, and sometimes k''x.

There are four clicks in Naron as in Nama:

| the dental or alveolar fricative click, formed by placing the front of the tongue broadly against the teeth or alveolus and releasing it with a soft, sucking sound.

! the retroflex plosive click, formed by pressing the tip of the tongue against the front palate and withdrawing it suddenly.

|| the retroflex fricative click, formed by placing the tip of the tongue broadly against the back of the palate and withdrawing it softly.

4-2

≠ the alveolar plosive click, formed as the retroflex plosive click, only with the front of the tongue far forward on the alveolus, almost on the teeth.

One hears variants of all these clicks; a person with a good ear might distinguish two or three of each kind. But such hair-splitting is neither necessary nor practical. The clicks vary automatically according to the vowel following, within certain limits: before i and e they are formed farther forward, before a, o, u correspondingly farther back. The distinguishing feature of each click lies more in the manner in which the tongue is pressed and withdrawn, than in the exact position in which it is placed.

Clicks, as all consonants except nasals, or s, ʃ, b, are only used at the beginning of a syllable, generally at the beginning of a word. Clicks may precede the vowel directly, or be followed by any guttural, or by n, h, or x. Most frequently they are followed by k.

Clicks occur most often in nouns and verbs. Pronouns, auxiliaries, and words in constant use rarely have them.

Tones.

According to the tone of voice in which a word is spoken, it varies in meaning. I have only been able to be sure of three tones. The medium tone I leave unmarked, the high tone I mark by a line preceding and above the word, the low tone by a line preceding and below the word. Thus:

te *me*, ⁻te *to step*; ₋ho *to come up, sprout*, ho *to marry*; !nuː *to build*, ⁻!nuː *far*; !xoː *a pipe*, ⁻!xoː *to pull, catch hold of*.

Nouns.

Nouns have the masculine, feminine or common gender.

The ending for the masculine is ba, shortened to b in proper names. Ba changes to m before the verb *to be*, before the possessive ending di, and before prepositions, thus:

kweba	*a man.*
kweme e	*a man (he) is.*
kwem-di	*a man's.*
kwem kwe	*with a man.*

Ba changes to tʃəra or tʃara in the dual, to tʃi, ʤi or ‖kwa in the plural. This last ending is only used for men or personified animals.

Feminine nouns end in sa or se, ʃa or ʃe, s only in proper names, changing to ʃara or ʃəra in the dual, and ʃi or si in the plural.

Common nouns have no ending in the singular, take khara in the dual, and ne, ni, or n in the plural:

kweba	*a man.*	kwesa	*a woman.*	kwe	*a person.*
kwetʃəra	(2) *men.*	kweʃəra	(2) *women.*	kwekhara	(2) *people.*
kwe‖kwa	*men.*	kweʃi	*women.*	kwene	*people.*

Kwekhara is particularly used to designate *a man and a woman.*

The masculine and feminine endings may be given to all noun roots, and their meaning is thereby altered. Anything particularly strong, or tall and slender, is masculine; anything small and weak, or round, is feminine:

> hi *any plant.*   hiba *a tree.*   hiʃa *a broad low bush.*

The right hand being the stronger hand is masculine, the weaker, left, feminine; in consequence all things on the right side of the body have become masculine, all on the left feminine:

tʃouba	*the right hand.*	tʃouʃa	*the left hand.*
ǂxeba	*the right eye.*	ǂxeʃa	*the left eye.*

Certain roots are, however, more often used with masculine endings, others with feminine. The common gender is not often used, save in words formed from xu: *thing*, such as ǂỹxu: *food,* kˑɔxo *meat.*

The possessive case is formed by adding di or ti to the nominative, in the masculine to the form in m:

duːba	*the eland.*	duːm-di	*the eland's.*
duːdʒi	*the elands.*	duːdʒ-di	*the elands'.*
!nuːʃa	*the hut.*	!nuːʃ-di	*the hut's.*
!nuːʃi	*the huts.*	!nuːʃ-di	*the huts'.*
xuː	*the thing.*	xuː-di	*the thing's.*
xuːne	*the things.*	xuːn-di	*the things'.*

There are no endings for nouns in the dative and accusative cases, which are either indicated by prepositions or more often merely understood. This makes the translation of Naron sentences very difficult, as they do not follow any special sequence of words. The object may stand first:

kwedʒi |gɔre ma ʃɛ, ‖nweba |gɔre ma ʃɛ, ‖mwem |kwa ‖neː.
Men prayer speaking send, (to) moon prayer speaking send, with moon talk.

Pronouns.

Personal pronouns have similar endings for gender and number to those of the nouns, except in the first person:

I	ti, tira, tire.	*we*	si, ʃi, sita, ʃita.
me	te.	*us*	ta, taːa.

The first person singular never shows gender, the first person plural rarely does so, si and ʃi being used for either gender according to the taste of the individual speaking. Whether the shorter or longer forms of the pronouns are used seems also a matter of choice. But in the plural there is a masculine and a feminine form that may be employed, namely: *we men* ʃi||kai, *we women* ʃiʃe.

ti ko |e: ||kamʃ ko !kũ.	*I (to) Fire Spring (Windhoek) have gone.*
ǂnu ⁻ka tire se ǂnaː.	*To-night I may dance.*
tira ka sana ǂnaː.	*I will dance later.*
au te ʃɔre.	*Give me tobacco.*
|geruba ko k'a te.	*The wasp bit me.*
!kũ ʃi tite.	*We do not go.*
ʃita ka xataxa kuru ʃɔren.	*We will also grow tobacco.*
ǂũ ta ko a tɔxo.	*Food we have put aside.*
si ||kai ko |giː i.	*We (men) do the dance.*
siʃe sana ⁻keixa.	*We (women) later grew up.*
ta ta ko ⁻mi.	*So we say,* or *so is said to us.*
Namani byri taːa.	*The Namaqua told us.*

The second person sa or ʃa takes the following forms:

		Masculine	Feminine	Common
Sing.	*thou*	satʃa, tʃa, tʃ	saʃa, ʃa, ʃ	—
Dual	*you*	satʃara, satʃau	saʃara, saʃau	sakhara
Plural	*you*	satʃi, tʃi, ʃa||kau	saʃi, ʃi, saʃau	ʃatuː, ʃa||kau

In the objective case sa is generally omitted and the ending alone used; this may be done in the nominative also, but is not so frequent:

satʃa ra ko ⁻mi.	*Thou (m.) hast said it.*
saʃa !kũ, tire !kũ tama.	*Thou (f.) goest, I do not go.*
tire ǂũ tite, ke tʃa ǂũ.	*I do not eat, but thou (m.) eatest.*
ʃa||kau wɛ||kau !kũ.	*You all go.*
ʃaʃau ka |eːre.	*You (women) can fetch wood.*
satʃi ||ga kwetʃi iː.	*You are old men.*
ʃatu _ha a ǂkumba ǂũ.	*You (c.) come to eat locusts.*
kwe tʃ ko |kũ, |noː tʃ ka ||oː.	*(If) thou (m.) killest a man, (by) war thou shalt die.*
ti ko ma ʃi.	*I told you (f. pl.).*
!xoba satu kuru.	*God made you (c. pl.).*
xaba ko |kũ tuːu.	*He kills you (c. pl.).*

The third person xa takes the following forms:

		Masculine	Feminine		Common	
Sing.	*he*	xaba, xam	*she*	xasa	*it*	xa
Dual	*they*	xatʃara		xaʃara		xakhara
Plural	*they*	xatʃi, xadʒi		xaʃi, xasi		xa‖kau, xan

In many cases the xa is omitted, and the ending alone attached to the verb, shortened to m, s, ʃ, etc. This makes confusion with the second person easy:

xaba ko |ni ⁻!nuː kwe ko ‖êi̅.	*He is living just over there.*
xam ǂā̃ ʃi, xaba ga ‖nei ʃi.	*(As) he knows them, he will talk of them (f.).*
e ko xasa ⁻‖kwi.	*And she contradicted.*
wɛana xa ko xauːe.	*(For) all one is tattooed.*
xan ‖kuŋ kwena ko byri taːa.	*They, the old people, told us.*
xatʃara-diʒi _kɔadʒi ti ko _!gwe.	*Both their karosses I carried.*
xaba ko dəbi, xaʃa ko dəbi, xakhara ko dəbi.	*He returned, she returned, they both returned.*
|kwane ko xaʃ |kwa ko _ha.	*The children came with her.*
‖k'au kwe |kwime ko ⁻muː ʃi.	*An Auen only sees them (f.).*
|garoba ko ǂniː i, ko ⁻m me.	*The ostrich turns and sees him.*
wɛdʒi xadʒi ko ⁻m.	*All of them (I) have seen.*
a ko ⁻tʃʌm dʒi.	*(He) steals up to them.*
xam-di !nu xa a.	*His house it is.*
kweba ko _dau tʃəra.	*A man burns them both.*
xas-ti ‖kunʃa ko ⁻|niːse ǂana ha.	*Her mother long ago knew that.*

As these examples show, xa in some ways corresponds to *that one*; it is often used with a noun, as *that, those*, for example:

a ko tira ⁻m xaʃ dẽʃa si |niːʃa.	*I saw that bow long ago.*
xa ⁻!nuː-dis xumʃa tam ka.	*That country's earth is like this.*

Perhaps one might best describe xa as the emphatic form of the third person; a non-emphasized nominative is omitted, while the objective is expressed by the noun-ending. The Naron have a habit of omitting the subject. Where no previous nominative has occurred, *I* is understood to be the subject. In telling a story, the person is mentioned in the first sentence, and then understood to be the subject of all following unattached verbs.

The possessive pronouns for the first and second persons singular are ti and sa, used as a rule without any ending. If the noun possessed is omitted, the possessive particle -di and the noun-ending are attached to the pronoun. The possessive pronoun for the first person plural is either sita or sita-di irrespective of gender. The second person plural hardly occurs, it would probably be formed with -di.

The third person is treated more as a noun, it always forms the possessive case with -di:

ti hoːba ko wɛxa kuru.	*My husband made them all.*
tira ga sa |kwa ⁻m.	*I want to see your child.*
|nis ǂgɔbeʃa ti-diʃa iː, sa ǂgɔbe tamaa.	*This bag is mine, thy bag it is not.*
ʃita ⁻!nuː kwe ra ko ⁻m ʃi.	*In our country I have seen it.*
ʃita-din ||kuŋ kwena iː.	*Our old people were (there).*

|ne, |niː *this*, |eː *some, any*, tã *other*, are declined as xa:

|neba !gume e.	*This one is short.*
|niʃəra ⁻tsu, |niʃəra !kãĩ.	*This one (of two) is bad, this one nice.*
⁻keiʤi dɔŋkiʤi ko _haː, |eːʤi kuːniʃa ko ||kɔri, |eːʤi ko !xwe.	*Many donkeys came, some drew the waggon, some ran away.*
Naman _!gwiʃa kuru, |eːn k'wiː, |eːn ⁻||oː.	*The Namaqua had smallpox, some recovered, some died.*
kwena ko _ha, ko ǂnumʃa ko ⁻xuː, a ||guː tãʃa.	*People come, uncover the ashes, light another (fire).*

ta, tas without the nasal, is used for the indefinite *so, thus*:

ta khara ko ko hĭ na.	*So the two did to them.*
tas ko ⁻mi.	*So it is said*, or *so she said.*
ta ta ko ⁻mi.	*So we were told.*

The reciprocal pronoun is ku:

||kaʤi ta ko ⁻||nɛː, a ko ⁻maː kuː, a ko ⁻khɔvi kuː, a ko ʃama kuː.	*Of goods we speak, give (them) to each other, visit each other, divide with each other.*

There is no relative pronoun.

Adjectives.

Adjectives may precede or follow the noun they qualify. They have no degrees of comparison. They are sometimes used without endings, sometimes declined as the noun:

Hiʃeʃa ko _ha ǂnuː ⁻ka, keiʃ ʃi ko ǂnuː iː; kwe kama sa iː tama, a |xeːʃa iː, a ǂxeːʃi |nya; !ga tam _iː ha, a !gum ǂaro |kwa.	*Hiʃeʃa came at night, then they were dark; like a person she was not, evil she was, with red eyes; tall she was not, with a short little body.*
tʃauba ⁻kei, tʃauba ||kuŋ ǂaro.	*The tail is long, the tail is broad.*
||axas ⁻keis.	*Old Axas (name of a woman).*
|nakak'aʃa |niːʃe, |xeːʃi iː, xabaxa ʃ tõĩʃi.	*A stick insect this is, bad they are but pretty.*

The numeral adjectives used by the Naron are:

|kwi: *one* |kʌm *two*   !nwɔna *three.*

One is declined as an adjective. *Two* may be used without an ending, or take the suitable dual termination. *Three* is not declined and seldom used; other numerals are never used save in counting up to please an investigator and they vary with each individual:

|kwi:m ko |kũe, num ko |kwi:m |xɔreba ko xaue.	*One (buck) is killed, then one tattoo mark is cut.*
|kwe ⁻kwe |kwi:ʃ |xɔʃa ra ko |kũ.	*At Kwes one gemsbok I killed.*
|kwi:m kweba |kwi:s kwesa ko ʃɛ.	*One man marries one woman.*
|kʌm ku:nen ko _ha:.	*Two waggons came.*
|kʌmtʃəra tʃɔk'autʃəra tʃɔʃa kuru.	*Two medicine men work magic.*
!nwɔna k'au kwe ko i:.	*Three men were there.*

|kwi: and |kwi:xa are used as *only* or *alone*:

k'umsa ||naum ⁻ka |kwi: ko nabo.	*Grewia berries in summer only (we) gather.*
k'au kwe |kwi:xa ko kuru.	*A man does it alone.*

Adjectives can be changed to adverbs by adding sə:

ǂnu: kwen ko byri ⁻ta tõĩsə si:se |hũ kwe.	*The black men spoke nicely to our master.*
|k'arisə ko misis a ko _kum.	*A little does Missis understand.*
xaba ko ⁻keisə !kũ.	*He runs fast.*

Otherwise there are no regular adverbs. Time is expressed by nouns or verbal particles, place by verbs or nouns with prepositions:

misis |na: ko !kũ; _!gwa ⁻ka ko kurikwas ⁻kwe ko ⁻ʃi dəbi a ga ||k'um, _kabaʃa !u: ⁻ka toe kɔbis ⁻kwe a.	*Missis this (day) has gone; at night to Kurikwas will come returning and will sleep, (the) new (day) at dawn will go on to Gobabis.*
kweʃ ⁻!nu: kwe i:.	*The woman is far off (in the country).*
|kõʃa ||ka tẽ.	*The owl flies up (ascending).*

The negative is expressed by tama or ta generally used after the verb:

wɛ kwe |gi tama.	*Not every man dances.*
tu:ʃa ko tu:, !gwi:ʃa ǂkai tama, !gwi:ʃa ko tẽ tama.	*(When) rain falls, a rope (trap) (I) do not sling, the trap does not rise.*

With the first person singular the negative may change to te with the short form of the pronoun:

!kũ tite.   *I do not go.*

Verbs.

Verbs are conjugated by means of verbal particles or auxiliaries which may precede or follow them. These alter for tense and mood, but not for person. Thus:

Present tense.

tira ⁻ma:	*I give*	sita ⁻ma:	*we give*
satʃa ⁻ma:	*thou givest*	satʃi ⁻ma:	*you give*
xaba ⁻ma:	*he gives*	xatʃi ⁻ma:	*they give*

or

⁻ma: ra ko	*I give, am giving*	⁻ma: ta ko	*we give, are giving*
⁻ma: tʃ ko	*thou, etc.*	⁻ma: tʃi ko	*you, etc.*
⁻ma: b ko	*he, etc.*	⁻ma: tʃi ko	*they, etc.*

Past tense.

tira ko ⁻ma:	*I gave, have given*	sita ko ⁻ma:	*we gave, have given*
satʃa ko ⁻ma:	*thou, etc.*	satʃi ko ⁻ma:	*you, etc.*
xaba ko ⁻ma:	*he, etc.*	xatʃi ko ⁻ma:	*they, etc.*

Future tense.

tira ka ⁻ma:	*I shall give, etc.*	⁻ma ra ḳa	*I shall be giving*

Subjunctive mood.

ne re ⁻ma:　*that (I) may give, etc.*

Passive voice.

The ending e attached to the active voice makes the passive:

tira xau　*I cut.*　　tira xaue　*I am cut.*

Most speeches are broken up into short clauses. The subject and verbal particle of tense stand in the first only, and are repeated by an indefinite a, a ko or koko before succeeding verbs:

tʃau ra ko k'aniʃa, a dɔ̃ɔ̃, a ‖k'um ʃi, a ǂũ ʃi.	*I dig ants, pick them up, sift them, eat them.*
‖naum ⁻kwe ta ko ǂũ ‖kanise, a ko ǀko, a ko tau, a ko ˍtum.	*In rain-time we eat nuts, pick them, stamp them, swallow them.*
ti ‖kunʃ ko ǀkwane aba, nos ka tira ǀgi, ‖gais ko i: ne.	*My daughter bears children, then I will name one, if a girl it is.*
ǀe:ʃ ⁻kwe tɔxo, ne i ‖ẽĩ.	*Put it on the fire, that it may burn.*
‖nweba ga (ka) ‖o:, a ga ⁻‖kai.	*The moon will die and arise.*

Conjunctions.

Conjunctions are not easily distinguished from verbal particles. Besides ne, ni *that, in order that, if,* there is ma which generally means *but*. Kai, ke mean *when, then,* and sometimes *but*. Xataxa usually can be translated *always*, xabaxa *however*:

|kwi: sa ko dəbi, ma ko |eani ⁻u.   *One returned home, but some went away.*

|ɛːʃa ko _karuː; kaim tama ʃ ko _ha, |niːʃ ko tʃəne; tʃənim koko ⁻kaː, ne _karu: ʃ ko.   *The fire is flaming; when no more is there, there (it) is baked; baking is not (possible), if it flames.*

|kũ ra ko, xabaxa re tire xaue tama.   *I used to kill, however I was not tattooed.*

ʃɔro a ko ||amiʤi ǂũ, ǂko ǂkoʤi xataxa ko ǂũ.   *The iguana eats ants, grasshoppers it also eats.*

Prepositions.

There are really only three prepositions, ⁻ka, ⁻kwe and |kwa *together with*. They always follow the word they govern. ⁻ka indicates time, ⁻kwe place, means, etc. !oː *the inside, the middle,* is often used with ⁻kwe as a preposition, which can be translated *among, inside, into, during.* Likewise k'ɛ *face, surface* is used with ⁻kwe as *on, upon.* Of course many other combinations are possible.

The Naron language, like all Bushman tongues, is most rich in verbs. They have one verb for *to put in,* another for *to put on,* another for *to put down,* and so on:

!u: ⁻ka xaba ka !kũ, ǂnu: ⁻ka ko _ha.   *At dawn he will go, at night he came.*

tʃəra ⁻||kai _|kwan ⁻!ku ⁻kwe.   *Both meet at Olifantskloof.*

|hũ |kwabəm-di ⁻kuːniʃa k'au-tʃas ⁻kwe a ko ⁻||kʌm a _ha.   *A white youth's waggon from Kautshas travelling came.*

a ko ||xaie !nabam ⁻kwe.   *(they) were beaten with a hide whip.*

me ko kwe ||ɛːxaba ||neiʃ !oː ⁻kwe ko _haba.   *Then the Bushman captain went to live among the tsama melons.*

k'aniʃa ko⁻ǂnu: |xərum k'ɛ⁻kwe.   *The ants sit upon the sieve.*

ǂaroasa ʃuːʃ ⁻kwe ǂkãe, a |nwiːasa |kwa tʃənxue.   *The body is put into a pot, and boiled with the fat.*

||k'au ||eba ko kuːni |kwa _ha.   *An Auen man came together with the waggon.*

Interrogatives.

The interrogative *who?* is diːna? *Whom? what?* and *which?* are duː? *Why?* is duːʃ !kaː ⁻kwe? or duːʃ !kau ⁻kwe? evidently a noun phrase, probably *for what reason?*

When? and *where?* are mʤa? or mtʃa?

diːna ko |ɛːane ɔaxa?	*Who brought the wood?*
xa xuː diːna ko kuru?	*Who made that thing?*
duː tʃa ko kuru?	*What are you (man) doing?*
duː ʃa ko kuru?	*What are you (woman) doing?*
duː xuːne ko ⁻uːwa _ha?	*Having what goods did (you) come?*
||eisa mdʒa?	*Where do you live?*
mdʒa tʃa xuː a _ha?	*Where do you come from?*
mdʒa kam ||eim |eːm kweba _ha?	*When did that man come?*
duːʃ !kau⁻kwe|kʌm |kwĩsera ko kau?	*Why do you two names give?*
tʃaʃa mdʒa?	*Where is the water?*

AUEN.

The Auen language is more clearly monosyllabic than Naron. Its phonology seems identical, but the intonation is peculiar. The Auen raise their voices higher and drop them lower than the Naron do. This gives their speech a carrying quality. A farmer who works with them told me, that the man ploughing with him will chat to a friend at the far end of the field, both speaking in their ordinary manner yet being distinctly understood. I know from experience that an Auen talking near by is far more disturbing than a Naron.

In Vedder's *Grammar* five tones are given for the Kung language. Very likely the Auen have as many, but I was unable to be sure of more than three, which I mark as explained on p. 52.

Nouns.

Auen nouns have no gender. To distinguish sex, when necessary, _||goː *male* and ⁻di *female* are added to the noun. The former can be used alone as *man*, but *woman* is dzou not ⁻di. *Right* and *left* are called *male* and *female* as in Naron:

_!goː	*ostrich*	_||goː _!goː	*male ostrich*	_!goː di	*female ostrich*
ʒuː	*person*	!kwã	*man*	dʒou	*woman*
!gou	*hand*	_||goː !gou	*right hand*	!gou ⁻di	*left hand*

There is no dual; the plural is formed by adding si or ʃi to the singular. Before *two* and *many* this ending may be omitted:

ʒuː	*person*	ʒuːsi	*people*	ʒuː ⁻tsa	*two people*
!num	*stone*	!numsi	*stones*	!numsi ⁻≠khi	*many stones*
dama	*child*	damasi	*children*	dama ⁻≠khi	*many children*

Cases are not marked by endings. The nominative precedes the verb, dative and accusative follow it, the dative first. The possessive is indicated by placing two nouns together, the possessor first. In a few terms of relationship the reverse is the case, with o in between:

!kwã kei hã ⁻tsa.   *The man has two horses.*
ha ⁻|ka au mi kuː.   *He does not give me milk.*
a ko |k'au guːme kuː.   *(He) milks the cow's milk.*
m⁻ba ⁻ba.   *My father's father.*
m_tai o dzou.   *My wife's mother (mother of wife).*

Pronouns.

The personal pronouns have no forms for masculine and feminine in the singular, but distinguish them in the plural, thus:

mihi, mi	*I*	e !ka	*we* (m.)
		ehe, e	*we* (f.)
ahi, a	*thou*	i !ka	*you* (m.)
		ihi, i	*you* (f.)
hai, ha	*he, she, it*	si !ka	*they* (m.)
		sia, si	*they* (f.)

The longer forms are the emphatic nominative: the shorter either nominative or objective. In the first person singular the objective can be changed to me or m.

The sign of gender in the plural is dropped when speaking of both sexes, and before *two* and *all*.

All personal pronouns can be used as possessive pronouns, but usually the short forms are employed:

mihi m, _ahi ⁻|ka m.   *I eat, thou dost not eat.*
hai ⁻!nuː.   *He stands up.*
e !ka ko ⁻u, ihi ko gɛː.   *We (men) go, you (women) stay.*
|hũ ⁻tsa tʃi se a, e ⁻|ka sɛ. *Two white men came, we did not see (them).*
mihi ku sɛː !nau, a ku |nʌm si. *I have seen the bow, I have played them.*
au mi, m ⁻u |aː a ke.   *Give to me, I go out to present to thee something.*
e oasi ku ⁻u.   *We all went out.*
i ⁻tsa m.   *You two are eating.*
m _tai a naro ⁻di, m ⁻ba a ||k'au ||ẽ. *My mother was a Naron, my father was an Auen.*
hwitib k'wi te ha _tai |kwi ⁻keis. *Hwitib calls his mother Big Kwi.*

The demonstratives tsiː, tsiːke, tʃiː, tʃiːke can be used as adjectives or pronouns:

mihi gu: tʃ'u a tsiːke.   *I take this house (house which here).*
ʒuːsi tʃiː ku tʃɔm ⁻kou.   *These people are gathering, picking.*
e o _kɔa tʃiː.   *We fear these.*

There is no real relative pronoun but adjectives and numerals are sometimes joined to the nouns by a or by o. These may be parts of the verb *to be*:

dɔnki o ⁻tsa te ⁻|ka ⁻ʃiː.   *Two donkeys have not come.*

Adjectives.

Adjectives are few. They follow the nouns they qualify and are not declined. The diminutive maː may be attached to other adjectives as well as to nouns. There are no degrees of comparison:

!nwiː ⁻zɛː	*new moon*	!nwiː ⁻≠ẽsi	*full moon*
!nwiː ⁻≠gaː	*old moon*	!nwiː _maː ⁻zɛː	*little new moon*
dama	*child*	dama !goːma	*little child*
dama !goːma o !kwama		*little child who a man, little boy.*	

Numerals.

The Auen only use |ne or |ne⁻e *one*, and ⁻tsa *two*, though they understand most of the Nama numerals. Both of these follow the noun, sometimes after o. |ne can also be used as *only*, or *alone*:

kuri |ne tʃ'u !khuː.	*One year the hut stands.*
ma a |ne⁻e ku ⁻tsi.	*I alone have come.*
_!kwã ⁻tsa ku ⁻tsi.	*Two men have come.*
ʒu |nwasi ⁻≠khi ku ⁻uː.	*Many Bushmen have gone.*

Verbs.

The root of the verb remains unchanged. Used alone it signifies the present or an indefinite tense. Other tenses are formed by verbal particles preceding the root. The principal ones are:

ko, ku	past tense.
ka	future tense.
re	continuous action.
a	a repetition of the tense in the preceding clause.
o	present, or an unfinished action.

mihi ⁻|niː.	*I stay.*
e o !goː.	*We are sitting.*
ha ko ⁻uː kurikwa.	*He has gone to Kurikwas.*
ʒuː ku kuru !num.	*A person has worked the stone.*
ha ka ⁻tsʼa, _kɔma ka ⁻tsi.	*He will sleep, to-morrow will come.*
si tʃiː o ⁻tsiː.	*These are coming.*
si ⁻≠khi re ku ≠kʌbi.	*Many of them were riding.*
|kʌm re ⁻kwi.	*The sun burns.*

Interrogative and Negative Particles.

Questions are asked by means of the particle ba which may be used with verbs and nouns. *Where?* is expressed by ba o kure? *Who?* is tʃaː ba? or tʃeː ba? These may also be used for *what?*

⁻tʃ'u ba o kure?	*Where is the hut?*
i tʃaː ba a kuru?	*Who did this?*
i tʃeː ba a ʃi tsi?	*Who has come here?*
a tʃeː ba ⁻ku?	*What is burning?*
a ⁻ʒu ba heː?	*What person is that?*
a ⁻ʒusi ba he?	*What people are those?*
ahi ba a sɛː ⁻ʒu?	*Have you seen the person?*
ǀkʌm a ⁻tsi re ba a ⁻tsi?	*The sun had come where you came?* (or) *Had the sun come when you came?*

Not is ⁻ǀka or ǀkwã̄ used before the verb. There are two negative verbs which are very much used, _kaː *not to exist*, and _kwara or _kɔra *not to be at a place*:

⁻ʒu ǀnwasi ⁻ǀka kuru.	*Bushmen do not make (it).*
mihi guːmi tʃiː,	*My oxen these,*
ǀkwã̄ o ahi guːmi.	*(they) are not your oxen.*
_kaː _dɔrosi.	*There are no leaves.*
ka ǃnumsi _kwara, ⁻ʒu o guː ǃgãĩsi.	*When stones are not there, a person takes bushes.*
ka ⁻ʒu _ǁgãũa, me o sɛː, kwe ⁻ʒu ǀũã; ka ⁻ʒu ko sɛː, e ka _kwara.	*When a person is a spirit, I see (it), like a man; then one sees (it), and then it is not there.*

Adverbs.

Adjectives are changed to adverbs by adding si. These precede the verb:

⁻ǃhaisi ⁻u.	*Go quickly.*
tsa ǀki re o ǁãũsi sɔː ka ǀeː.	*That thing must roast long in (there).*
_ǃnwiː ⁻ma ǃmsi ⁻ʃuː.	*The new moon lies nicely.*

Many expressions denoting time are similar to those of the Naron. They are mostly nouns with ⁻ka or ke, and stand in any part of the sentence.

Place is denoted in much the same way:

ǁnwɔi ⁻tʃiː ⁻ǁkai ke, ko m i _ǃgwa tsiː ⁻ka.	*The jackal comes to-day, eats this evening.*

_!gwa ‾ka kuru, a ka _kɔma ‾ka ‾sɔ:.	*To-night I make (it), and to-morrow will bake (it).*
|wixamab !nœre o kwi: ke.	*Wixamab's country is here.*

Conjunctions.

The Auen generally break up their speech into short clauses strung together without conjunctions: yet a few such exist:

ka, kam, kama	*when, as, if, because*
xabe	*but, although*
na	*that, and*
kesi	*and, also*

kama !ga: o |nʌm, ‾ʒu o tʃanə.	*When rain has fallen, one dances.*
mi ‾|ka sɛ:, kama m a dama !go:.	*I did not see, because I was a little child.*
|a:, na mihi m.	*Give, that I may eat* (or) *Give, and I eat.*
m _tai kesi ‾ba.	*My mother and father.*
k'ari k'ausi ‾|ka m, xabe si kau !nwe: m.	*The youths did not eat, but they could eat later.*

Prepositions.

Besides ‾ka and ke used after nouns, generally corresponding to *at* or *in*, there are no real prepositions. Sometimes the connection between verb and noun is simply understood, sometimes a verb of motion, such as \|\|a *to pick up*, !ko: *to set down*, ‾\|u: *to fill in*, etc. is used after the chief verb:

sɔ:e _dɑ:a.	*Roast in the fire.*
‾ʒu |u: ‾|gu:.	*A person fills in water.*
gu: tʃi:, !nɔ̃: ‾|u: !kũ:.	*Dig a hole, throw in the ants.*
|kabe ‾di ‾tsa ri !ko:.	*Two Bechuana women are sitting.*
hi ku !name !ko: tʃi:a.	*They fall into the hole.*

A comparison of Auen and Kung speech (see Vedder's *Grammar*), will show the close relationship of the two. I read some Kung tales to the Auen, who caught the meaning, but would correct the sentences, either altering the pronunciation, mostly by a change of click or vowel, or substituting another verbal particle, or occasionally a root word.

The Auen language is slightly more like Naron than the Kung language is, which one would expect from their being near neighbours.

I much regret that I could not fix in writing half the tones they used in speaking.

NUSAN.

The very small amount of this language I was able to collect, makes it difficult to give any grammar. All rules must be accepted as taken from a very limited number of examples.

The phonology is similar, but with a smaller use of labials and dentals, a larger use of gutturals and clicks. Among the latter is the fifth or labial click marked ⊙. This click sounds like a kiss. It can only precede a labial or h.

The nouns have different forms for the plural. I find a few reduplications, a number with the endings te, atə, ni, nə, rə and some with singular and plural the same:

Singular	Plural	
tuː	tutuː	*person*
ǁkã	ǁkãte	*horn*
ǁkam	ǁkamatə	*thorn*
ǂũ	ǂũni	*eye*
ǀk'a	ǀk'arə	*hand*
ǁõĕ	ǁõĕnə	*crow*
ǁnei	ǁnei	*hut*

There is no ending for the dual, but some nouns do not take the plural ending after *two*, as tuː !num *two people*, tutuː ǁkari *many people*.

The position of the noun shows its case; the subject precedes the verb, the object follows it:

si se ɛ̃ _ha.   We will eat food.

I find no trace of gender in nouns or pronouns.

For purposes of comparison I give a list of the personal pronouns side by side with those of Colonial Bushman speech:

	Nusan	Colonial Bushman
I	ŋ, m	ŋ, m, ka
thou	a	a
he, she, it	ɛ	ha, he
we	si	i (incl.), si (excl.)
you	i	u
they	u	he, hi

In the emphatic form the pronoun is doubled, giving ŋ-ŋ, a-a, ɛ-ɛ, si-i, i-i, u-u. The short form is also used as possessive pronoun.

The numerals are !koe, *one*, !num *two*, ǁgãĩ *three*. They follow the nouns.

The verb is conjugated by means of verbal particles preceding it. The vocabulary has many words similar to those in Colonial Bushman.

I think even this brief outline of the grammar of these three tribes will show my reason for dividing Bushmen into three groups. The fact that the Northern Group is more like the Southern than the Central, and lies grammatically between the two, in contradistinction to the geographical distribution, is remarkable. The Central Bushman Group on the other hand approaches Nama, and almost belongs to the Hottentot tongues. How comes this?

The Hottentots are supposed to have come down from the Great Lakes in the north-east. Did they come down the Ngami road, spreading out to the south-east thereof, subduing the Bushman inhabitants of the Central Kalahari and forcing them to use their language? If so, they passed while yet in a primitive state themselves, for they left no signs of culture, no flocks and herds among their sometime servants. Also they must have passed on long enough ago, to give time for a separate language to form itself.

Or are the Naron a tribe of undeveloped Hottentots, showing us what the latter were, before they received that admixture of blood, and made that step in civilization from hunter to herdsman, which distinguish them from the Bushman?

Did the Naron, pressed by the Bantu, follow their stronger kinsmen from the north-east, as the latter divided the Northern and Southern tribes in their advance?

It is all conjecture, but a fascinating subject.

List of Plants used as Food, etc.

Compiled with the help of Miss Wilman, *Curator of the McGregor Museum, Kimberley.*

PLANTS OF WHICH THE FRUIT IS EATEN.

	Naron	ǁk'au ǁɛn
Ehretia hottentottica, Burch.	ǁk'auba	
Grewia cana, Lond.	k'um	⁻ǃniː
Grewia flavescens	ǃko ǁkuba	
Tragia duoica, Lond.	⁻tʃiː ǃgani	_dɑni
Methania rupestris, Schinz	ǃkeima	
Coccinea sessillifolia	ǀgəri	toa
Cucumis africanus, L. f.	tʒa	tʒa
Trochomeria debilis, Hook f.	ǃgum ǀu	
Corallocarpus Welwitchu, Hook f.	ǀhɔro	ǀkɔro

PLANT OF WHICH THE LEAVES ARE POUNDED AND EATEN.

	Naron	‖k'au ‖ɛn
Talinum caffrum	ǂãsi	‖k'ãsi

PLANTS OF WHICH THE ROOT IS EATEN ROASTED.

Dipcadi glaucum, Baker		‖ka
A *Scilla* species	‖a⁻bi	ǀkwe

PLANTS FROM THE ROOT OF WHICH LIQUID CAN BE OBTAINED.

Raphionacme Burkei, N. E. Br.	biɛʃa	ǂe ‖aː
Acacia glandulifera, Schinz	ǀk'arə	ǀk'arə

PLANT OF WHICH THE ROOT IS USED AS MEDICINE.

Indigofera alternans, D. C.	k'ɔko	k'ɔko

PLANT OF WHICH THE ROOT IS USED AS A CHARM FOR SHOOTING.

Rhynchosia totta	kawab	kwɔbo !gau

HERBS USED FOR TOILET AND CEREMONIAL PURPOSES.

Lepidium ruderale, L.	tʃã	tsã
Ocimum fruticulosum, Burch.	tʃã	tsã
Peliostomum leucorhizum, E. Meyer	tʃã	tsã
A *Sutera* species	k'au tʃã	tsã
Bouchea pinnatafida, Schauer	tʃãba	ǀaua ‖ẽ
Epaltes gariepina, Steetz	ǀgərə ǀgɛː	tsã
Hibiscus Elliottiae, Haro.	ǀkau ‖na	tsã

PLANT OF WHICH THE LEAVES ARE USED FOR SNUFF.

Waltheria indica, L.	‖gãĩ	!gwã

PLANT OF WHICH THE FIBRE IS USED FOR MAKING ROPE.

Sansevieria zeylanica, Willd.	⁻!gwiːba	⁻!gwiː

GRASS USED FOR THATCHING.

Schmidtia bulbosa	ǀgã	‖khi

GRASSES USED FOR MAKING CHAINS FOR NECK AND WRIST.

Scirpus nodosus, Rottb.	‖kuŋ ‖wa	
Kyllinga alba	ǀk'weẽ	⁻gɔri